RETURN TO
GLORY

A HISTORY OF THE GEORGIA BULLDOGS

LORAN SMITH

FOREWORD BY KIRBY SMART

RETURN TO GLORY: A History of the Georgia Bulldogs®

Whitman
Publishing, LLC
PUBLISHING SINCE 1934

Table Of Contents

DAWG FANS ARE CHAMPIONS, TOO!

With any successful venture, there will always be many unsung heroes and behind-the-scenes vignettes that complement the headline makers. Such as Ryan Williams, graduate assistant, who suggested the running back pass for the College Football Playoff Semifinal at the Orange Bowl. We didn't have a lot of success with it in practice, but, at that propitious moment in Miami, it worked to perfection to put us up 14-0 over the Michigan Wolverines and gave us reassuring momentum.

You always appreciate the players who buy into the team concepts and work selflessly to claim the prize. That is what Coach Erk Russell wanted to achieve when, in 1980, he came up with those tee shirts that said, **BIG TEAM, little me**. If you don't put the team first, you are not likely to win a championship, especially a national championship.

That is why I have always appreciated the Georgia fans. What a fan base we have! Our coaches who come from other places have noted right off just how well our fans travel.

There are many loyalists and contributors who are deserving of a high five with our championship run during the '21 season, but I want to especially thank our fans.

Bulldog fans follow us everywhere with intense passion. It was mind blowing at how our fans took over Notre Dame Stadium when we played there in 2017. That was overwhelming, and it gave us a home game feeling.

And the Rose Bowl. That was a little bit understandable in that having an opportunity to go there in a semifinal playoff setting would stimulate the most exciting response imaginable. Nonetheless, our players and coaches naturally took note of how many of our fans found their way into this iconic stadium.

Our fans are so vocal, and it obviously comes from the heart. It is fun to see them tailgating and having elevated fun wherever we play. While television makes it easy to enjoy football in one's own den, the loyal fans, who make the effort to travel with the team and "help" their team to victory, have become a vital part of the college football landscape. I certainly hope we never lose that.

We are constantly aware that our fans are attracted to out-of-town venues to enjoy the local flavor. Our fans, and I am sure that is the way it is with other SEC schools, love going to Nashville, Music City, USA. Dawg fans really appreciate the horse farms and the Bluegrass environment when we play Kentucky in Lexington.

We don't play LSU that often, but when we do, New Orleans becomes a must for Dawg loyalists. The French Quarter becomes dominated by red with constant shouts of "Go Dawgs."

They enjoy excursions to Jacksonville, Columbia, Auburn, Tuscaloosa and Oxford. They are anxious to journey to College Station, Austin and Norman when the SEC schedule takes us those iconic college towns.

Most of all, we appreciate our fan base for their making Sanford Stadium the place to be on fall Saturdays. Our student section lustily cheers us on, our fans from Clayton to Bainbridge, from Ringgold to St. Marys have invested into our program with commitment and feeling. Such fan support makes a difference, and I am proud to say that our fans are the best. Go Dawgs!

- *Kirby Smart*

Head coach Kirby Smart holds the College Football Playoff National Championship trophy during the University of Georgia campus celebration inside Sanford Stadium on January 15, 2022. Photo by Mackenzie Miles.

THE EARLY YEARS

"A good fist-fight was an integral part of a hotly contested game."

—John Stegeman

It all began on January 30, 1892, when Mercer University agreed to come to Athens to play Dr. Charles Herty's newly formed team. It wasn't much of a contest, with the home team's biggest challenge being removing rocks and smoothing out the surface of the mostly grassless gridiron. Georgia won 50-0 at a time when a touchdown counted four points, and the kick after, two points.

Herty, a Georgia graduate who'd received his Ph.D. from Johns Hopkins, was one of the most important men in the history of the University of Georgia and in the state itself. It was he who'd introduced football to his alma mater—but perhaps more significantly, he was the renowned chemist who developed the process from which paper is made from wood pulp. The pages of this book are the result of the genius of the first football coach at the University of Georgia.

After the win over Mercer (it was a two-game season, with Georgia losing 10-0 to Auburn in Atlanta), the progress of football in Athens went nearly two decades without distinction. Georgia went through 12 coaches before Alex Cunningham took over in 1910 and boosted Georgia's football reputation considerably.

One of those 12 coaches was to become one of the great names in college football in the first half of the 20th century: Glenn "Pop" Warner. In 1896 he fielded Georgia's first undefeated (4-0) team.

When Warner coached against John Heisman, then at Auburn, little did the spectators know just how important these two men would become to college football. And who was on hand to cover Georgia games early in the 20th century? None other than the *Atlanta Journal*'s Grantland Rice, who was on his way to New York and recognition as one of America's preeminent sportswriters.

(Preceding page) Georgia's football team of 1894 had five wins with one loss to Sewanee in Athens. Coach Robert Winston, standing upper right, was the university's first paid coach. An Englishman, Winston had previously coached rugby before coming to the United States to train football teams at Amherst, Rochester, Syracuse and Yale. (Right) A graduate of Cornell University, Glenn Scobey "Pop" Warner, top, began his 44-year career as a head coach at the University of Georgia. In 1896, the 25-year-old Warner guided the team to its first undefeated season at 4-0.

BULLDOGS

1892-1927

BULLDOGS

Pop Warner, a Cornell graduate, began his coaching career at Georgia, but stayed only two seasons. The year after he left, there was great excitement in Athens because of a versatile young quarterback, Richard Vonalbade ("Von") Gammon of Rome, Georgia. But in the Georgia-Virginia game on October 30, 1897, at Brisbine Park in Atlanta, Gammon charged from 15 yards behind the defensive line of scrimmage and collided with the Virginia interference. He crashed to the ground on his chin with great downward thrust, causing what would be a fatal brain concussion.

Von Gammon's name will be forever etched in Georgia football history because of his mother's impassioned plea that his death would not bring about a state law to ban the playing of football.

Gammon came from a family with great affection for the outdoors and physical activity. It was only natural that he would take to football when he enrolled at the University of Georgia. His passion for exercise and fitness was so fervent that people claimed not to recognize him in street attire. Gammon was usually to be found in his training clothes.

Von Gammon's death came at a time when there was a great national outcry to legislate football out of existence. More than a few politicians and educators preferred that the game be rendered null and void. In 1896, at least 27 players were killed across the nation by football-related injuries.

The passion to abolish football after Von Gammon's death ran feverishly high in Georgia. A bill banning the sport was overwhelmingly passed by the Georgia House and Senate. Only the governor's signature was needed to put an end to football once and for all in the state of Georgia.

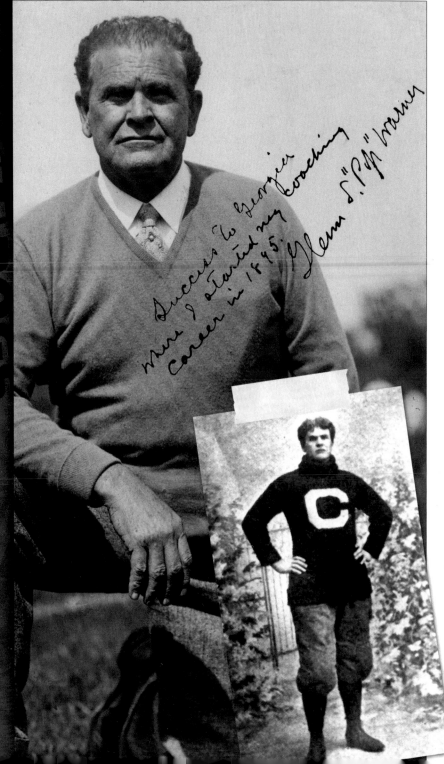

Success to Georgia. Where I started my coaching career in 1895. Glenn S. "Pop" Warner

After leaving UGA, Pop Warner embarked upon a long and illustrious career in college football, coaching at his alma mater Cornell (inset), Carlisle Indian Industrial School, University of Pittsburgh, and Stanford University. When this photo was taken in 1933, Warner had just accepted the head coaching position at Temple University, a position he would hold for five years. He was inducted into the College Football Hall of Fame in 1951, passing away three years later at the age of 83.

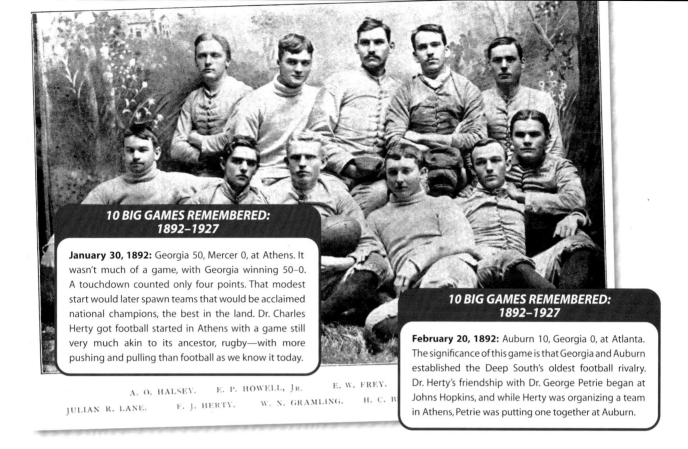

10 BIG GAMES REMEMBERED:
1892–1927

January 30, 1892: Georgia 50, Mercer 0, at Athens. It wasn't much of a game, with Georgia winning 50–0. A touchdown counted only four points. That modest start would later spawn teams that would be acclaimed national champions, the best in the land. Dr. Charles Herty got football started in Athens with a game still very much akin to its ancestor, rugby—with more pushing and pulling than football as we know it today.

10 BIG GAMES REMEMBERED:
1892–1927

February 20, 1892: Auburn 10, Georgia 0, at Atlanta. The significance of this game is that Georgia and Auburn established the Deep South's oldest football rivalry. Dr. Herty's friendship with Dr. George Petrie began at Johns Hopkins, and while Herty was organizing a team in Athens, Petrie was putting one together at Auburn.

A. O. HALSEY.   E. P. HOWELL, JR.   E. W. FREY.

JULIAN R. LANE.   F. J. HERTY.   W. N. GRAMLING.   H. C. B

Herty weighed in with an open letter to the *Atlanta Journal,* suggesting that one of the problems for football at Georgia was the lack of facilities for proper training. "Regret over the Von Gammon disaster is general and sincere, but the degree to which some strictures go is unreasonable and unjust," he wrote.

When Von Gammon's mother, Rosalind Burns Gammon, saw Herty's letter, she wrote Governor W.Y. Atkinson,

It would be the greatest favor to the family of Von Gammon if your influence could prevent his death from being used as an argument detrimental to the athletic cause and its advancement at the university. His love for his college and his interest in all manly sports, without which he deemed the highest type of manhood impossible, is well known by his classmates and friends, and it would be inexpressibly sad to have the cause he held so dear injured by his sacrifice. Grant me the right to request that my boy's death should not be used to defeat the most cherished object of his life.

(Top) In 1892, Georgia's first team was coached by chemistry professor Charles Herty. Herty had become enamored of the game while he was a graduate student at Johns Hopkins University. In February of that year he agreed to play Auburn, whose team was coached by his friend and former classmate George Petrie. That historic game sparked the South's oldest football rivalry. (Far left) Dr. Charles Herty. (Left) This leather helmet is typical of those worn by college players throughout the early 1900s.

The governor yielded to Mrs. Gammon's plea and refused to sign the bill, thus preserving football in the state of Georgia—a decision that undoubtedly had an influence on the preservation of the game nationally.

Not forgotten in this regrettable incident is the legend of Gammon's response after the collision that would result in his death. As he was being taken off the field in a state of semi-consciousness, a defiant Von Gammon reportedly said, "A Georgia man never quits."

(Above) After being soundly beaten 10-0 by Auburn in 1892, Georgia rallied to a 10-8 win in Atlanta in 1894. (Far right) This poster could be found all over Atlanta in the days leading up to the 1894 Georgia-Auburn game. Georgia was captained by quarterback George Butler (right).

GEORGE BUTLER,
Captain of the University of Georgia Team

Foot Ball!
Great Annual Thanksgiving Day Interstate Contest—Georgia and Alabama.

University of Georgia
VERSUS
Auburn.

On Buffalo Bill's Wild West Grounds, Just Outside Exposition Grounds.

Thursday, November 28th

Game Called at 12 O'Clock, sharp; Over by Two O'Clock.

Commodious Grand Stands, and Carriage Entrance.

Take Southern Railway Cars at Markham House.

Admission 50c. Grand Stand 25c. Extra

Colors: University of Georgia, Red and Black. Auburn, Orange and Blue.

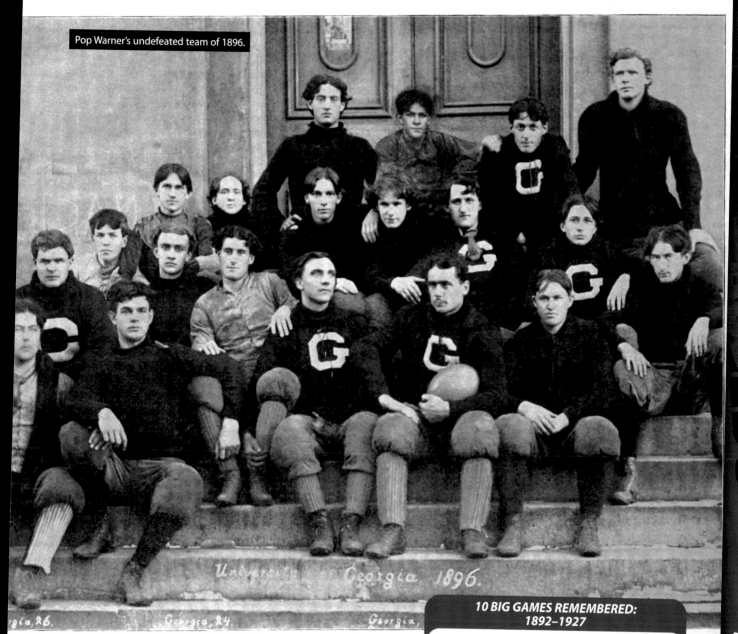

Pop Warner's undefeated team of 1896.

University of Georgia 1896.

Georgia 26.   Georgia, 24.   Georgia,

10 BIG GAMES REMEMBERED: 1892–1927

October 26, 1895: North Carolina 6, Georgia 0, at Atlanta. This game is where many say the forward pass originated. In a kicking situation, the Carolina punter, in desperation, "flung the ball forward over the scrimmage line into the arms of a startled teammate," who raced for a touchdown. The referee allowed the illegal play to stand, saying he "didn't see it." Scouting the game, Auburn's John Heisman later wrote to Walter Camp, the recognized rules authority at the time, recommending that the forward pass become legalized "in order to open up the game." In 1906, the forward pass was officially made legal.

November 26, 1896: Georgia 12, Auburn 6, at Atlanta. Another first involving a Georgia team took place. Auburn appeared to have caught on to Georgia's signals. It was at this point that Georgia dropped behind the line of scrimmage while the quarterback gave a signal out of earshot of the Auburn team. This move on Georgia's part later gained widespread credit as college football's first huddle.

In 1897, quarterback Richard Vonalbade "Von" Gammon (left) tragically died from a head injury sustained during UGA's hard-fought battle against Virginia. His death produced outraged cries that the barbaric game be outlawed in Georgia. Von Gammon's mother, Rosalind, wrote to the governor pleading that "my boy's death should not be used to defeat the most cherished object of his life." (Below) A handsome bronze plaque honoring Mrs. Gammon's sacrifice is today displayed beneath the rotunda of Butts-Mehre Heritage Hall.

In the early 1900s, Georgia games were still being played on North campus. There was no spectator seating, and the playing surface was little more than bare earth. From the outset, the big games were played in Atlanta. Since the team was transported via train, playing in Atlanta was easier for players, team officials, and spectators alike.

One of the most distinguished players after the turn of the century was Harold "War Eagle" Ketron, of Clarkesville. John Stegeman wrote in *The Ghosts of Herty Field* that, to Ketron, "a good fist-fight was an integral part of a hotly-contested game." According to Stegeman, Ketron's physician father didn't take kindly to that sort of conduct. He came close to denying his son the option to compete in football at the university after reading about the young man's involvement in a free-for-all in 1902. Ketron lettered in '01, '02, '03, and '06, and was captain of the 1903 team. After Georgia experienced the loss of several players in one season, the *Atlanta Constitution* wrote of the team's prospects the next year, "Fortunately, Ketron is a whole team by himself."

Ketron would become an invaluable football recruiter while pursuing his professional life as a Coca-Cola bottler in Wilkes-Barre, Pennsylvania. He was responsible for sending Charley Trippi, Joe Geri, Joe Tereshinski, and others to play for the Bulldogs.

When Georgia played its early games, there were no bleachers, and spectators stood along the sidelines. Some arrived by horse and buggy to take in the action. As the game grew in popularity, the need for a more advanced spectator facility became apparent.

In 1911, Sanford Field was constructed from a swampy bog at the bottom of Lumpkin Street, though it was intended to accommodate baseball more than football. Bordered by wooden grandstands along the foul lines, it was an attractive venue for baseball, the money sport at that time.

Nonetheless, Sanford Field doubled as the home of the football team, which gave Georgia an inferior

---

10 BIG GAMES REMEMBERED: 1892–1927

November 19, 1910: Georgia 11, Georgia Tech 6, at Atlanta. Led by Bob McWhorter, a four-year winning streak against Georgia Tech began, ending the frustration of losing to the teams of legendary John Heisman (first at Auburn and later at Clemson). When Heisman moved to Tech, his teams had beaten Georgia for 15 years. Georgia won 11–6, and a grateful and joyful celebration began.

When the team of 1910 posed for this photograph, the lens captured several UGA "greats," including: soon-to-be university president Steadman Sanford, standing far left; Georgia's first All-American, halfback Bob McWhorter, standing fourth from left; future head coach George "Kid" Woodruff, seated fourth from left; and head coach William A. Cunningham, front row, far right.

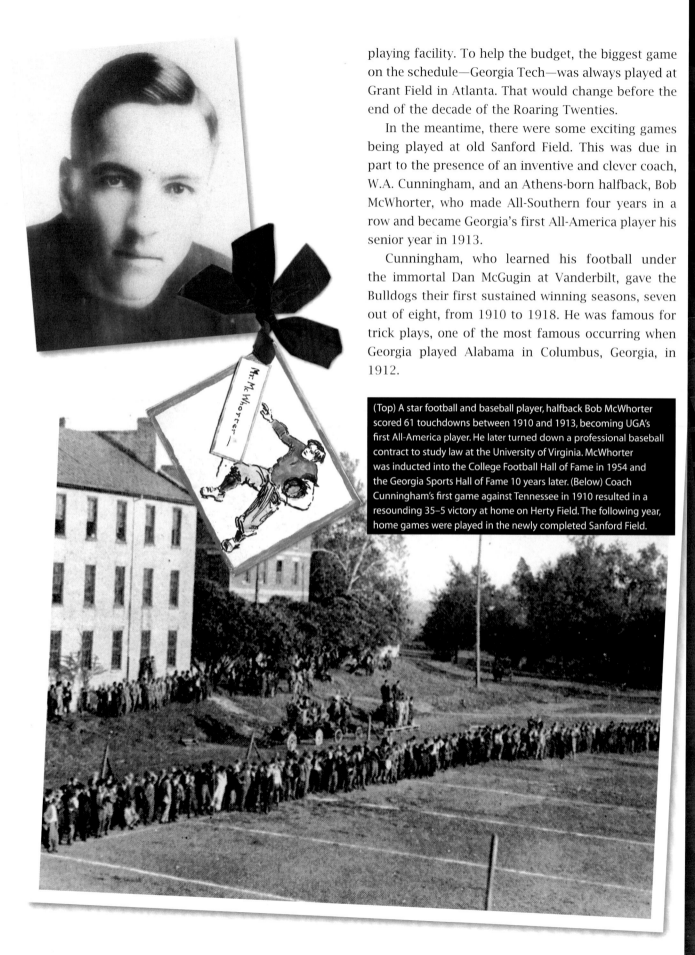

playing facility. To help the budget, the biggest game on the schedule—Georgia Tech—was always played at Grant Field in Atlanta. That would change before the end of the decade of the Roaring Twenties.

In the meantime, there were some exciting games being played at old Sanford Field. This was due in part to the presence of an inventive and clever coach, W.A. Cunningham, and an Athens-born halfback, Bob McWhorter, who made All-Southern four years in a row and became Georgia's first All-America player his senior year in 1913.

Cunningham, who learned his football under the immortal Dan McGugin at Vanderbilt, gave the Bulldogs their first sustained winning seasons, seven out of eight, from 1910 to 1918. He was famous for trick plays, one of the most famous occurring when Georgia played Alabama in Columbus, Georgia, in 1912.

(Top) A star football and baseball player, halfback Bob McWhorter scored 61 touchdowns between 1910 and 1913, becoming UGA's first All-America player. He later turned down a professional baseball contract to study law at the University of Virginia. McWhorter was inducted into the College Football Hall of Fame in 1954 and the Georgia Sports Hall of Fame 10 years later. (Below) Coach Cunningham's first game against Tennessee in 1910 resulted in a resounding 35–5 victory at home on Herty Field. The following year, home games were played in the newly completed Sanford Field.

John Stegeman described perhaps the most notorious sleeper play in Georgia history:

> On the first scrimmage play, a quarterback, Alonzo "Hooks" Autrey, hid out on the sideline. It was understandable that Alabama failed to notice him since he had on civilian clothes and held a water bucket in his hand. As the ball was snapped, Autrey dropped his bucket, ran down under a long pass, and came close to scoring before a wide-eyed Alabaman tackled the speeding water boy just short of the goal.
>
> Immediately, a general riot suspended play for over half an hour. During the melee, Professor John Morris, standing in for Athletic Director Steadman Sanford, was approached by his Alabama counterpart. "In the name of sportsmanship," Morris was told, "ask Coach Cunningham to recall the play." When the professor refused, he was flattened by the Alabama athletic director.

(Above) Former Vanderbilt player William A. Cunningham coached the Bulldogs from 1910 to 1919. Before his arrival, the 13-year-old UGA football program had seen 13 different head coaches. Cunningham is often credited with bringing both continuity and success to the team, producing seven winning seasons with a compiled coaching record of 43-18-9.
(Top left) When Coach Cunningham returned to Georgia after serving in World War I his 1919 Bulldogs ended the year at 4-2-3. Here, Georgia battles it out with Alabama. The following year, Cunningham rejoined the army as a career officer, eventually attaining the rank of general.

When Coach Cunningham's Bulldogs beat Georgia Tech 20–0 in 1912, this cartoon depicted Tech's coach John Heisman pleading for mercy.

10 BIG GAMES REMEMBERED: 1892–1927

October 26, 1912: Georgia 13, Alabama 9, at Columbus. Coach Alex Cunningham hid quarterback Hooks Autry on the sideline in street clothes, carrying the water bucket. When the ball was snapped, Autry dropped the water bucket and ran downfield to catch a pass. He was stopped short of the goal, and a 30-minute brawl ensued. Order was restored and Georgia was the winner. This was Georgia's most notorious sleeper play in an era when rules were not firmly established.

When cooler heads prevailed, the teams began to play football in earnest, with Georgia winning a thrilling encounter 13-9.

Georgia's first business manager of athletics, Charles Martin, remembers the story differently. He recalled that Autry wasn't too keen on playing the role of "sleeper." It had nothing to do with ethics but the fact that he had a date with a girl after the game and had only one pair of trousers. "Whenever it became evident that he was going to be tackled near the goal line," Martin said, "Hooks simply stopped and lay down, thus preserving his trousers if not gridiron glory."

McWhorter never lost to Alabama or Georgia Tech. A former mayor of Athens, he was a longtime member of the law school faculty. His greatest regret was that Georgia never won the Southern Conference championship while he was on campus, but he brought the little town of Athens enough football glory to firmly establish that the fortunes of the football team would annually affect the emotions of the populace. His accomplished performances stimulated hopes that Georgia could compete well enough to bring championships to the supporters of the Red and Black. McWhorter was the first of several Athens natives who would lead the Bulldogs to honor and glory on the football field, and in 1954, he became the first Georgia player elected to the College Football Hall of Fame.

From 1917 to 1918—Cunningham's late years as a coach—Georgia did not field a team because of World War I. Tech, however, did field a team and became the butt of a considerable number of jokes about Tech students avoiding the military while practically every able-bodied Georgia student volunteered. In the baseball series of 1919, Georgia students produced parade floats that featured Georgia students in foxholes in the Argonne Forest and Tech students on Grant Field. Tech complained that its patriotism had been impugned, and the two football teams would not compete again until 1925.

10 BIG GAMES REMEMBERED: 1892–1927

November 16, 1912: Georgia 20, Georgia Tech 0, at Atlanta. Along with Bob McWhorter, the star was quarterback Dave Paddock in this third straight victory over Tech. After the game, a spectator walked up to Paddock and extended a warm greeting. "It is an honor to shake the hand of a great player," the gentleman said. It was baseball legend Ty Cobb.

When Cunningham rejoined the army as a career officer, his assistant, H.J. Stegeman, succeeded him. Stegeman, who'd played for the legendary Amos Alonzo Stagg at Chicago University, had been sent south by the army after World War I to organize a physical training program for the university's ROTC department.

After settling down in Athens, Stegeman applied for a coaching job and became an assistant football coach. With Cunningham's departure—and owing to a glowing endorsement from Stagg—Stegeman became the head coach of football, baseball, basketball, and track. He would later become athletic director as well as dean of men.

A full-blooded Dutchman from Holland, Michigan, Stegeman was an innovative athletic official. In addition to having creative ideas, he had contacts throughout the country and the connections to get things done for the betterment of Georgia athletics.

(Below) In 1917 and 1918, UGA suspended its football program when America entered the war. Fifteen players and two coaches immediately signed up for military service. In 1919, Georgia played its first three games after the war at home at Sanford Field, which served double duty as the university's baseball and football stadium. (Right) As a student at the University of Chicago, Herman J. Stegeman played football on the school's 1913 National Championship team under illustrious coach Amos Alonzo Stagg. After WWI, he was hired as assistant coach at UGA. When Cunningham gave up football to return to the army, Stegeman became head coach. He served in that position from 1920 to 1922 with a 20-6-3 record, before stepping down to become the school's athletic director. A doting father, he is pictured here in 1922 with daughter Joanna and son John.

One of his greatest admirers, Dan Magill—long-time Bulldogs coach, sports information director, and historian—considers Stegeman to be Georgia's greatest athletic director. "The legendary football coach at the University of Chicago, Amos Alonzo Stagg, called Herman James Stegeman the greatest all-round athlete he ever coached," Magill says. He adds,

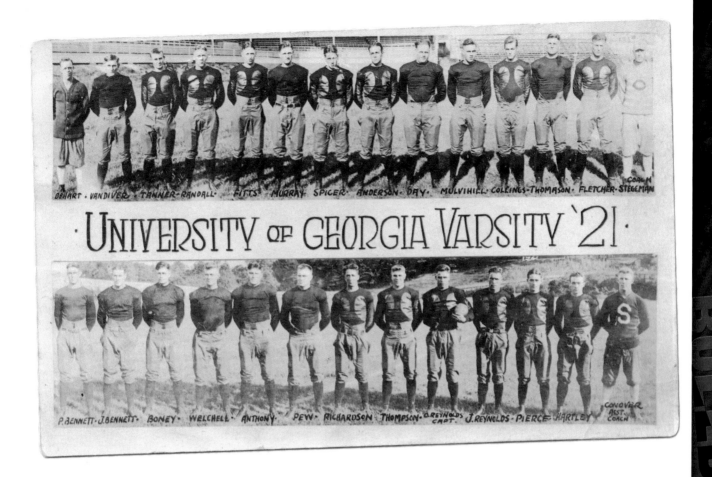

BEHART · VANDIVER · TANNER · RANDALL · FITTS · MURRAY · SPICER · ANDERSON · DAY · MULVIHILL · COLLINGS · THOMASON · FLETCHER · STEGEMAN COACH

·UNIVERSITY OF GEORGIA VARSITY '21·

P. BENNETT · J. BENNETT · BONEY · WELCHELL · ANTHONY · PEW · RICHARDSON · THOMPSON · O. REYNOLDS CAPT. · J. REYNOLDS · PIERCE · HARTLEY · CONOVER ASST. COACH

Coach Stege also was the University of Georgia's greatest all-round coach. His 1919 Georgia baseball team won the old Southern Conference title, and so did his 1920 Georgia football team. The last team he coached (track) won the Southeastern Conference title, then he retired as UGA athletic director and became dean of men. Stegeman Hall, home of Georgia's basketball games, appropriately is named for him, because he was the father of basketball in Dixie. He originated the first Southern Conference basketball tournament in 1921 at the Atlanta Auditorium, and it flourished there through 1932. The Southeastern Conference originated the next year and Georgia won the basketball title with boys "Stege" had coached in 1932,

his last year as basketball coach. He was the first Southerner named to the National Football Rules Committee, being appointed by the chairman, his old coach, Stagg. He was responsible for Georgia playing its first inter-sectional football games, originating the Yale series at New Haven in 1923, and he was responsible for Yale coming South for the first time in the dedicatory game of Sanford Stadium in 1929. He also originated the old Southern Collegiate golf tournament at the Athens Country Club in the 1930s. He died unexpectedly from a heart attack at the age of 48 in 1939. His assistant, William Tate, who'd starred in track under Stege, succeeded him as dean of men.

It was Stegeman who brought the first football championship to Athens during his first year as coach. His 1920 team won eight games and tied Virginia in Charlottesville, 0-0. This was good enough for the old Southern Conference title.

It would be seven years before Georgia won another championship, and it had a bittersweet ending. George "Kid" Woodruff, who had gained fame as a smallish quarterback (hence his nickname), followed Stegeman as football coach and agreed to coach the Bulldogs for a dollar a year. His mission: take Georgia to the Rose Bowl.

In 1927 he put together a quick and speedy team that became known as the "Dream and Wonder" team. In the finale at Grant Field, his fast and shifty backs were slowed by a field that had been turned into a quagmire.

(Below) Coach Stegeman's 1921 team only lost two games, to Eastern powers Dartmouth and Yale, pictured here. (Below right) George "Kid" Woodruff followed Stegeman as UGA head coach, and he would lead the Bulldogs to the 1927 national title.

10 BIG GAMES REMEMBERED: 1892–1927

November 20, 1920: Georgia 21, Alabama 14, at Atlanta. With the score tied 14–14, Alabama lined up to kick the winning field goal with seconds left in the game. Puss Whelchel, who blocked 19 kicks in his career, blocked the Alabama attempt, allowing Buck Cheves to return the ball 85 yards for the winning touchdown. Georgia had its first championship.

COACH "KID" WOODRUFF

Georgia entered the Tech game having scored 248 points while yielding a total of 23 points to the opposition. Six teams were shut out.

Reports of what happened pregame say that, even though heavy rains descended on Atlanta late in the week, Tech added to the quagmire by further watering down the field. The fast Bulldog backs were stopped by the Tech defense and were upset 13-0.

Nauseated by the Tech victory, Dr. Steadman V. Sanford, Georgia's president and perhaps the Bulldogs' biggest fan, set in motion a plan to build the finest football stadium in the South.

Sanford, with absolute faith in the Georgia people, went to alumni and fans, asking them to sign notes for $1,000 to guarantee the cost of construction. The loan, originally set at $150,000, was increased to $180,000. Those who signed notes were given the right to purchase six tickets for any game inside the 40-yard lines. The response was overwhelming.

Even though the Great Depression hit in the fall of 1929, none of the notes signed by the guarantors was ever called. The strength of the Georgia family, "the majority party" in the words of Dan Magill, loyalist nonpareil, has never been more graphically demonstrated.

The stadium was dedicated on October 12, 1929. In that game, end Catfish Smith scored all 15 points and the Bulldogs upset mighty Yale and its star half-back, "Little" Albie Booth.

Following the 1927 season, during which Georgia was still acclaimed national champion, Kid Woodruff returned to his home and business enterprises in Columbus.

Woodruff, who helped form the Georgia Student Educational Fund (which was to become critically important for the financial health of Georgia athletics in the 1950s and beyond), had provided noteworthy contributions to his alma mater as coach. His salary of $1 a year was no burden to the budget, which was always in need of resources. He came within one game of getting the Bulldogs to the Rose Bowl, and

10 BIG GAMES REMEMBERED: 1892-1927

October 8, 1927: Georgia 14, Yale 10, at New Haven. Georgia was victorious because of gallant defensive effort in the second half. In desperation, Yale completed a long pass that appeared to bring about victory, but when the hay that had been put on the field because of bad weather was removed, the ball was two yards short of the goal line. Georgia had its first victory over Yale.

(Top right) When Georgia beat Yale for the first time ever during the 1927 National Championship season, joyful crowds swarmed College Avenue just outside the campus gates. (Right) The Georgia Redcoat Band.

(Above) Coach Woodruff's team on the practice field. (Right) All-America end Chick Shiver captained the 1927 National Championship team. (Opposite page) The 1927 title team, Woodruff's last as head coach, pose on Sanford Field.

his 1927 team beat Yale for the first time, 14–10, at New Haven. For a man named "Kid," those were giant accomplishments in Georgia football history.

Assistant coach Harry Mehre, the Notre Damer who was the center on the team that featured the fabled "Four Horsemen," took over. It was his chance to win the Southern Conference championship and get the Bulldogs to a bowl game.

The obsession of those who resided in dear old Athens town was for Georgia to play in a bowl game. Mehre fielded good teams, but bowls and championships were not yet to be.

December 3, 1927: Georgia Tech 13, Georgia 0, at Atlanta. The undefeated Bulldogs of 1927 were expecting a bowl trip to Pasadena, California, when wet weather caused a quagmire and Georgia Tech came away with a big upset. It was the most important defeat in Bulldog history in that it so incensed Georgia fans, it led to the development of Sanford Stadium.

NEXT: Harry Mehre comes to Athens. The Bulldogs get a new stadium. Beating mighty Yale.

THEY STILL REMEMBER THE OLD COACH

1928–1937
RECORD: 59 WINS, 34 LOSSES, 6 TIES

It was a brand-new stadium and a new day for Georgia, signaling that the Bulldogs were ready for big-time competition.

In the 1920s, throughout the country there was a coaching trend toward hiring former Notre Dame players. The Notre Dame box formation was the system that most colleges sought to install. What better way to emulate the Irish system than to hire a player who had learned from the master, Knute Rockne?

Georgia's hiring of Harry Mehre meant the school had an assistant who not only knew how to run and coach the Notre Dame system, but also was a colorful and witty coach. Later in life, Mehre became a popular after-dinner speaker.

Forrest "Spec" Towns, who won the Olympic high hurdles in Berlin in 1936, also played end on the football team. Following his gold-medal-winning race at the Olympics, Towns was invited (coerced, he would later say) to tour Europe and run a series of exhibitions. In Oslo, Norway, Towns set the world record of 13.7 seconds in the 110-meter high hurdles, a record that stood for 14 years.

Mehre sent Towns a telegram saying, "Minor sports are over, come home."

Once, after a Georgia basketball game against Kentucky, the Wildcats' legendary coach, Adolph Rupp, complained vehemently to Mehre about what Rupp considered a lousy performance by the referee. "Adolph," Mehre deadpanned, "I wish you wouldn't talk about my brother-in-law like that."

Mehre became a columnist for the *Atlanta Journal-Constitution*. His analyses were insightful and clever, just as his colorful commentary was when he was on his feet speaking to an eager audience.

(Preceding page) Late in 1927, Steadman Sanford asked the Georgia alumni and friends to guarantee a bank loan funding construction of a new football stadium with the promise that they would be awarded lifetime seats. The plan worked, and he raised $150,000 toward "building a stadium bigger than Tech." When Sanford Stadium was completed in 1929, it boasted a seating capacity of 30,000, with construction costs exceeding $300,000. (Right) In 1903, Sanford arrived at UGA as an English instructor. Nearly 30 years later he was named president of the university, eventually becoming chancellor of Georgia's university system. A visionary supporter of athletics, Sanford played a key role in forming the Southern Conference and its eventual offshoot, the Southeastern Conference. Today, Sanford Stadium proudly bears his name.

BULLDOGS

1928–1937

BULLDOGS

One day I walked down the aisle where Coach Mehre sat in the old press box at Sanford Stadium. Coach Mehre summoned me and said, "Listen, listen out there. They still remember the old coach. How nice it is that they keep calling out my name, 'Coach Mehre, Coach Mehre.'" It wasn't long before I could make out the Coca-Cola carrier boys sounding forth with "Cokes here, Cokes here." Mehre once told a big tackle that he had a charley horse between the ears. When another player was summoned to re-enter a game, he told Mehre he couldn't move his left shoulder. "Use your right one," an exasperated Mehre replied.

Using his sardonic, sarcastic style on the football field, Mehre would correct mistakes with the most graphic of explanations.

Mehre played for Rockne in Notre Dame's heyday. He was the center on the team that featured the immortal "Four Horsemen." One of his banquet stories had to do with the motivational skills of Rockne. In a critical moment, Rockne sent Mehre into the game, telling him, "Harry, if you make a bad pass, I'm going to kill you." Now that's real motivation!

After Georgia defeated Yale 15-0 in the Sanford Stadium dedicatory game, Mehre always joked that he was given a lifetime contract. Verbal of course. When he left for Ole Miss following the 1937 season, Mehre quipped, "They declared me legally dead."

Mehre had enjoyed above-average success at Georgia with a 59-34-6 record, but he never won the Southern Conference championship. Furthermore, he failed to coach the Bulldogs well enough to get to the Rose Bowl, the big objective of the local fans. However, he fielded teams that would have been good enough to go to bowls—like his 1931 and 1933 teams, both posting 8-2 records—if there had been more bowls available. The Orange Bowl's first year was 1933. The Sugar Bowl and the Sun Bowl played their first games in 1935.

Mehre was good at beating Tech, losing only twice in a 10-year span. There were two ties, including one in 1937 when Bill Hartman, captain and All-America fullback, ran back the second-half kickoff for a touchdown.

Harry J. Mehre played center at the University of Notre Dame, graduating in 1922. The following year he went on to the NFL, playing for the Minneapolis Marines. In 1924 he was offered a position at the University of Georgia as assistant coach, accepting the head coaching position four years later upon Coach Woodruff's retirement. During his 10 years at UGA, Mehre compiled a 59-34-6 record.

But what Mehre is remembered for is the Yale game on October 12, 1929. Coach Herman Stegeman, UGA's athletic director, and university president Steadman Sanford were able to persuade the Elis to come south to dedicate the stadium. The Bulldogs had played Yale six times, but all games had been played in New Haven. The first Georgia team to beat Yale was Kid Woodruff's 1927 team, which won 14-10, a noteworthy and prestigious accomplishment. Mehre lost to Yale his first season as head coach in 1928 but then proceeded to beat the mighty Easterners five games in a row, the only home game being the dedicatory game.

Sanford and Stegeman had held out hope that Yale would accept the invitation to play in Athens, but it was not a quick decision. It was the first time Yale had ever ventured out of the East for a game.

Yale had become the scourge of the East and rolled into Athens the heavy favorite, headlined by Albie Booth, a halfback with highly regarded credentials.

In 1928, the Bulldogs beat Tulane 20-14 (upper left) Furman 7-0 (upper right) and Mercer 52-0 (middle left). That same year, Sanford Stadium was being constructed, primarily with convict labor (left), which at the time was a common practice for the construction of public works projects.

In 1929, the Georgia Redcoat Band played before 30,000 fans at the dedicatory game of Sanford Stadium.

10 BIG GAMES REMEMBERED: 1928–1937

October 12, 1929: Georgia 15, Yale 0, at Athens. Mighty Yale came south to dedicate Georgia's new stadium. Fans came from all over the South, and Catfish Smith was all over the field, scoring all 15 points in a big upset. Georgia had the finest stadium in the South, and the first game between the then-infant hedges brought about an unforgettable victory.

Georgia, featuring the "Flaming Sophomores" (several players, such as linemen Red Leathers and Red Maddox, were redheads), wasn't given much of a chance in the game. The Bulldogs had lost to Oglethorpe 13-6 in the opener, something that depressed Georgia fans at the outset.

Mehre's wife, Hallie, the sister of former Georgia quarterback M.E. (Buster) Kilpatrick, was shopping at the big department store Michaels and overheard a woman say, "Look at her buying all that stuff. Her husband lost to Oglethorpe and has no chance against Yale on Saturday."

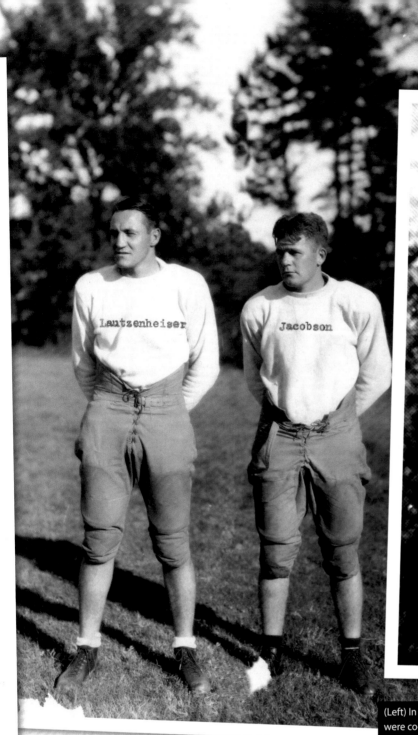

(Left) In 1928, tackle Glenn Lautzenheiser and end Roy Jacobson were co-captains of Coach Mehre's first team at UGA. (Right) Milton "Red" Leathers was one of the stars of the Bulldogs' sensational 15-0 victory over mighty Yale in 1929. In 1933, Leathers became the first Athens native to accept a position with the NFL when he went to play for the Philadelphia Eagles.

When the final gun sounded, it was Yale that had no chance, as the Bulldogs completely dominated the game. Mainly it was Vernon "Catfish" Smith who dominated. He scored all 15 points in an upset that had one New York newspaper proclaiming, "Catfish 15, Yale 0."

That game and his catchy nickname propelled the Macon native to All-America honors and would later serve as his ticket into the College Football Hall of Fame.

Several years ago, in order to video-document the scoring plays of the '29 Yale game for the Georgia

Over 30,000 fans attended the October 12, 1929, Sanford Stadium dedication game in which Georgia shut out highly regarded Yale 15-0. Perhaps the newly planted little hedges around the field had something to do with it.

archives, I took Catfish, in his late years, down to Sanford Stadium for a walk-through recall of where and how he scored all 15 points: recovering a blocked punt by Bobby Rose in the Yale end zone for Georgia's first score, then kicking the extra point, and catching a pass from Spurgeon Chandler—who went on to become an ace pitcher for the New York Yankees and the American League's most valuable player in 1943—for a touchdown. (Catfish missed the point after the kick.) He also threw Yale's heralded Albie Booth for a safety.

Catfish threw Booth to the ground with such extra force that the offended Booth was prompted to get up disgustedly and growl, "That doesn't go around here." With that, Catfish retorted, "No, Albie, it's you who doesn't go around here."

As we walked the field, he eagerly recalled how it was on the day that the entire nation focused its attention on the Georgia-Yale game in Athens. It was a brand-new stadium and a new day for Georgia, signaling that the Bulldogs were ready for big-time competition.

Yale came to town confident, having defeated Vermont 89-0 the previous week. At a banquet the night before the game, however, Red Maddox made such an emotional speech that a Yale coach whispered to Harry Mehre, "We're licked."

John Stegeman and Robert Willingham Jr. note in their book *Touchdown* that 27 trains brought 5,000 visitors to town on Friday. Sixty private planes landed at Ben Epps Field. "Governors, senators, congressmen, generals, and presidents of universities arrived from dozens of states," they write. "Most of the country's famous sportswriters were in town, as were the officials and personnel of the National Broadcasting Company, which was to beam the game to the rest of the nation. All 30,000 of the stadium's seats were sold long before October, and 3,000 aisle and standing-room tickets went on sale the morning of the game."

When Yale arrived that Friday by special train, thousands of citizens and officials met the visitors. They sang the Yale "Boola, Boola" fight song to welcome Yale to town. The Yale band then paid tribute to Georgia by playing "Hail to Georgia Down in Dixie."

Center Joe Boland was the captain of the 6-4-0 1929 team.

10 BIG GAMES REMEMBERED: 1928–1937

October 11, 1930: Georgia 18, Yale 14, at New Haven. This was the second game of a five-game winning streak versus Yale, but it looked bleak for the Bulldogs. In the press box, Grantland Rice began writing his lead for a Yale victory. Catfish Smith then caught a long scoring pass to reduce the deficit to 14-12. In the last minute, Georgia reached the Yale six. Quarterback Austin Downes handed the ball to Jack Roberts, and the big fullback scored to shock the Yalies again.

BULLDOGS

1928–1937

10 BIG GAMES REMEMBERED: 1928–1937

November 8, 1930: Georgia 7, NYU 6, at New York. Georgia had two fine ends in Catfish Smith and Herb Maffett, but Catfish's catchy name often gave him the lion's share of the spotlight. Maffett was clearly the star in this game and scored the tying touchdown. Catfish kicked the winning point. New York papers headlined the next day: "Catfish Smith beats NYU 7 to 6."

To my friend
Loombs,
Vernon "Catfish" Sm
b. 1 de. 1931

The game began with Yale kicking off. Georgia would gain the upper hand early on, and Stegeman and Willingham put into focus how the Bulldogs of Georgia conquered the mighty Bulldogs of Yale, considered the University of Georgia's mother institution:

Austin Downes, Georgia quarterback, fielded the kickoff at his 20, returning 17 yards. The Sanford Stadium era was underway. Georgia got little yardage in two plays and Vernon "Catfish" Smith, one of the seven sophomores in the starting lineup, dropped back from his end position to punt. The ball traveled only 29 yards.

Georgia's strategy was to lure Yale into a punting duel, with the Bulldogs' Smith kicking on first, second, and third downs, with expectations of getting the better of it. But the plan backfired as Smith averaged but 22 yards on his first four punts. If anyone in the press box was looking for a "goat" at that stage of the game, Catfish Smith would have been the choice.

With each of Smith's short punts, Yale found itself ever nearer to the Georgia goal. But making first downs was a different story; they came with extreme difficulty. All the while the sun was bear-

(Preceding page) Rumor has it that All-America Vernon "Catfish" Smith got his unusual nickname when a fellow Macon high school student bet him that he would not bite the head off a catfish. Between 1929 and 1931 Catfish enjoyed a sterling football career at UGA before going on to coach at Georgia and the universities of South Carolina and Mississippi. Later in life, he was inducted into both the Georgia Sports Hall of Fame and the College Football Hall of Fame. (Below) Built into a gentle ravine running between UGA's Old Campus and Agricultural School, newly constructed Sanford Stadium can be seen in this rare photograph beside old Sanford Field, the former home of Bulldog football from 1911 to 1928.

10 BIG GAMES REMEMBERED: 1928–1937

October 10, 1931: Georgia 26, Yale 7, at New Haven. Georgia's tiny halfback, Homer Key, broke open the game with a 76-yard run, with every player on the Yale team gallantly trying to hem him in. Guard Red Leathers scored Georgia's first touchdown on an interception. Against Yale in those years, the South rose again.

10 BIG GAMES REMEMBERED: 1928–1937

November 7, 1931: Georgia 7, NYU 6, at New York. For the second year in a row in Gotham, the Bulldogs were 7–6 winners. Before the game, Buster Mott predicted he would return the opening kickoff for a touchdown. Mott didn't even start the game, but Coach Mehre, on a hunch, started Mott in the second half. Mott responded by returning the kickoff 95 yards for the touchdown that enabled the Bulldogs to claim victory.

(Above) All-America quarterback Austin Downes (carrying ball) was influential in beating Yale for the second year in a row when the Bulldogs went to New Haven in 1930. (Left) Former head football coach Herman Stegeman served as the University of Georgia's athletic director from 1923 until 1937. When Stegeman Hall was demolished in preparation for the 1996 Summer Olympics, UGA's basketball facility was later renamed Stegeman Coliseum in his honor.

10 BIG GAMES REMEMBERED: 1928–1937

December 1, 1934: Georgia 7, Georgia Tech 0, at Athens. Alec Ashford established himself as the greatest 145-pound end in Bulldog history. Often outweighed by 75 pounds, Ashford, nonetheless, was a terror on defense. On Tech's best drive, he smeared the Jackets' 220-pound Jack Phillips for a 17-yard loss. Said Tech coach Bill Alexander, "Painful as it is, I love to watch that little guy play."

ing down, and the Yale players, in their dark-blue woolen jerseys and long blue stockings, began looking longingly for the water boy.

Guard Milton "Red" Leathers recalled that the Georgia line, taking a tip from Herman Stegeman, who had scouted Yale, over shifted on every play to the Yale strong side. "They could have killed us with a reverse," said Leathers, "but it was early in the season and they had not installed a reverse in their attack. Every play was run to the strong side where we were bunched, waiting for them. We spent much of the afternoon in their backfield."

Weddington Kelly, another sophomore end, remembered the turning point. "During a huddle in the second quar-

(Above) Bulldog end Graham Batchelor was also a UGA track star.

In all of the excitement of the game, not a lot of overt attention was paid to the foot-high shrubs that encircled the playing field. These were the infant hedges that Charlie Martin had planted. When the hedges matured, not only did their aesthetic appeal add to the consummate beauty of Sanford Stadium, but they elicited feeling and affection from the followers of the Red and Black and drew praise from visitors who were smitten by the stadium's appearance. Eventually "Between the Hedges" came to mean a Georgia home game, where the Bulldogs developed a reputation of being difficult to beat.

Georgia would finish the important 1929 season 6-4. It would be remembered for the dedication of the stadium and the coming of the Great Depression in a few weeks. One of the sweetest victories following the dedicatory game was whipping Georgia Tech 12-6 between the infant hedges in late November.

No longer would Georgia travel to Atlanta every year to play Tech on Grant Field. When the two teams met from that point on, the Bulldogs would no longer defer home-field advantage to the Yellow Jackets. The ignominious insult that was the Tech upset of the 1927 national champions eventually paid off; Sanford was spurred to lead the effort to build the stadium that bears his name. And there was an emotional bonus that came with the building of the

ter," he said, "someone—I can't remember who—said in a somewhat surprised tone, 'You know what I think? I think we can beat this bunch!' That would have sounded like idle chatter at the beginning of the game but now it gave us a big boost."

Dan Magill has written that, although Sanford was willing to give Yale half the gate receipts for its consideration to come south to help draw a big crowd, the Yale president took only expenses, which is what Georgia had been receiving when the Bulldogs traveled to New Haven to play the Elis.

10 BIG GAMES REMEMBERED: 1928–1937

October 19, 1935: Georgia 13, N.C. State 0, at Raleigh. A pregame free-for-all and John Bond's punting were the highlights. Bond punted nine times for a 44-yard average, which greatly influenced the outcome. The pregame fist fight spawned an eye-for-an-eye-and-tooth-for-a-tooth battle on the field. Tackle Allen Shi won most of his battles, but when he went down with a groin injury, Wolfpack fans rose and cheered. "It was the only standing ovation I ever got," Shi said afterwards.

BULLDOGS

1928-1937

BULLDOGS

(Top) The Bulldog team of 1937 was the last coached by Harry Mehre. The old coach went out in style, however, beating Miami a whopping 26-8 during the last game of the season. (Left) In 1934, the Southern Bulldogs beat the Eastern Bulldogs for the fifth consecutive year. (Above) Louis Elwood Wolfson, a former Bulldog player of the early 1930s, was a wealthy Wall Street financier and thoroughbred race horse breeder.

classiest stadium in the South: it would be five long years before Tech beat Georgia again.

Mehre fielded teams that contended for the Southern Conference championship—1930, 1931, 1933, and 1934—but always came a game or so short of attaining that goal. In 1931, the Bulldogs were a contender for a Rose Bowl invitation, but a 20-7 loss to Tulane in Athens derailed hopes.

Then, in the final game of the year in Los Angeles, Southern Cal embarrassed the Bulldogs 60-0. When the train brought the Bulldog team into Atlanta, Mehre wanted to make a local call, which then cost a nickel, but he didn't have any change. He said to Coach Stegeman, "Let me borrow a nickel, I need to call a friend." Stegeman flipped him a dime and said,

"Here's a dime, go call all of them." Football attitudes are fickle and have been since long before television replay and computers gained prominence with the game.

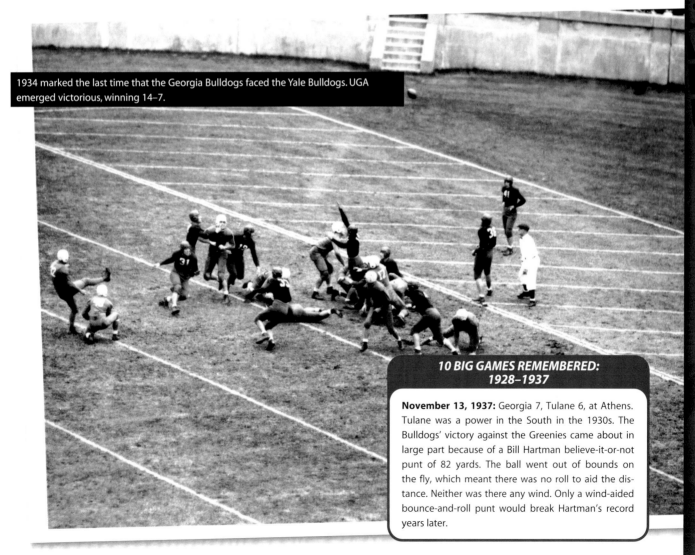

1934 marked the last time that the Georgia Bulldogs faced the Yale Bulldogs. UGA emerged victorious, winning 14–7.

Georgia's intersectional games spiced the schedule and enhanced the Bulldogs' reputation. Players like Joe Boland, Herb Maffett, Harvey Hill, Tommy Paris, and Tiger Bennett would distinguish themselves after graduation. Add to that group Cy Grant, Butch McCullough, Pinky Townsend, John Bond, and Andy Roddenbery. Many of them fit in the category described by Dean William Tate: "There's nothing finer than a Georgia boy with a Georgia education."

Those men were proud of playing Between the Hedges and were proud, too, of their education.

Louis Wolfson, a former Bulldog player, had became a wealthy industrialist who gave generously to Georgia athletics. He made an offer to buy the Baltimore Colts in the 1950s, but only if his long-time friend Wallace Butts would coach the team. "We made him an offer we didn't think he could refuse," said Louis Trousdale, Wolfson's assistant. Butts did refuse, however.

Mehre experienced a losing season in 1932 but bounced back with an 8-2 team again in 1933. From that point on, his teams declined in win-loss totals from seven to six to five.

---

10 BIG GAMES REMEMBERED: 1928–1937

November 27, 1937: Georgia 6, Georgia Tech 6, at Atlanta. This would be Harry Mehre's last Tech game. Hobbled by injury, Bill Hartman returned the second-half kickoff 93 yards but missed the point-after kick. When Tech scored later, defeat was avoided when Quinton Lumpkin blocked the extra point. Rules then allowed the kicking team to run blocked kicks over the goal line for the point after. Lumpkin then kept Tech's returner from the end zone with a devastating tackle, slamming him across the track, thus twice keeping Tech from victory on the same play.

Guard Elijah Pope "Pete" Tinsley was the first Bulldog to be selected through the NFL draft process as we know it today. After graduation, Tinsley played for the Green Bay Packers from 1938 to 1945.

In 1936, the Bulldogs whipped the Gators 26-8, due in part to the extraordinary efforts of No.10, Glenn Johnson.

He had players like John Bond and Andy Roddenbery, who helped him win games against NYU and Yale. Without a doubt, there was a feeling among his players that the South should rise again when they met those teams north of the Mason-Dixon line. Mehre was not above identifying with the Southern sense of pride. Before the Fordham game in 1936, Mehre, according to John Stegeman, said to his team: "The Yankees came through Georgia and burned and pillaged your homes, molested your women, and kept your grandparents in bondage for years. Today we have the opportunity of avenging the entire South against the descendants of those people who victimized your families and homes."

The team charged out to the field and tied favored Fordham 7-7, knocking them out of a Rose Bowl invitation. One of Fordham's prominent linemen was none other than Vince Lombardi.

Playing like a madman, as he often did, Pete Tinsley helped raise the victory flag. Victory is what Fordham coach Jimmy Crowley, one of the Four Horsemen who had coached with Mehre as an assistant, suggested after the game. He brought the game ball to the Bulldog dressing room and said, "It's yours, you won it."

Tinsley went on to play for the Green Bay Packers for six years. A native of Spartanburg, South Carolina, he returned to the South in the off-season for years. Eventually, he settled permanently in northern Wisconsin, where he taught school. He married a Wisconsin girl who settled him down from his wild days in Athens. He lived in Florence, Wisconsin, an area he came to love passionately. An avid fisherman, he spent his golden years fishing to his heart's content.

He often visited the Packers for reunions and alumni gatherings. When Lombardi became the Packer coach, Pete went up to him one day and reminded him of the 1936 tie. "Hell yes, I remember that game," Lombardi growled. "How could I ever forget missing out on the Rose Bowl?"

When I visited Pete in his Wisconsin home, he said of the conversation: "Lombardi was cordial at first, but as soon as I mentioned our game with Fordham, he changed the subject. He had no interest in talking about the game."

Pete was as famous for brawling and fighting as he was for making blocks and tackles. He would take all comers and usually was the last one standing. There are wild stories about people breaking chairs and

Forrest "Spec" Towns came to UGA in 1933 after he was offered a track scholarship. He also played end on the football team. After winning the 1936 gold medal for high hurdles at the Berlin Olympic games, Coach Mehre sent him a telegram reading, "Minor sports are over, come home."

ketchup bottles over his head. "It didn't matter how unbelievable the story sounded, it was probably true," Bill Hartman said.

In my conversation with him late in his life, he told a story about hanging around the downtown eatery The Varsity one evening when some players with Northern addresses brought up the Civil War. Pete said he told them, "All we needed was a few more rifles and a couple of sacks of parched corn and we would have whipped you."

BULLDOGS BATTLE TIGERS TO SCORELESS TIE

TECH vs. GEORGIA

GRANT FIELD
SATURDAY --
2 P.M.

CAPT.
SIMS

CAPT.
HARTMAN

With that, he exclaimed, "You boys ain't so tough." Then he took a razor blade, slit the flabby part of his jaw, and poked a lit cigar through the split and puffed away. "Those Yankee boys couldn't take it. One of them fainted and the others turned and ran."

Nobody ever questioned Pete's toughness. Neither did they question the toughness of Quinton Lumpkin, whose fight with Pete was supposed to have shaken the earth surrounding the New College building, where the players lived.

Lumpkin played center and backed up the line. He was as muscled as Charles Atlas. In high school, he won the state 220-yard dash. Admirers respectfully called him a "beautiful athlete."

In 1937, Mehre's last year, the Bulldogs and Tech fought to a 6-6 tie on Grant Field. Although hobbled with an injury, Bill Hartman, the captain, returned the second-half kickoff 93 yards for a touchdown. Winded from the run, Hartman, who was pressed into kicking duty with the regular kicker sidelined, missed the extra point.

It was a game that could have been lost when Tech later tied the score—except for Quinton Lumpkin. "He

(Above) Coach Mehre's last game against Tech in 1937 ended in a 6-6 tie in Atlanta. Georgia was captained by future College Hall of Fame fullback Bill Hartman.

saved the game not once, but twice," note Stegeman and Willingham. He blocked the extra point, but the rules in those days allowed for the ball to be picked up and run over the goal line for a point. Tech's Marion "Dutch" Konemann picked up the blocked ball and began sprinting toward the goal. Lumpkin met him at the one-yard line and knocked him sprawling all the way across the cinder track. It was a lick that Pete Tinsley cheered.

Although it would not be known immediately, Mehre's career was over. Not so for the career of his star back, Bill Hartman. The All-America fullback from Madison would not dress out again for the Bulldogs, but after a year with the Washington Redskins, Hartman, who had married a campus beauty queen, Ruth Landers, returned to Athens as the backfield coach for Wallace Butts.

It was the beginning of a long and altruistic career that ended when Hartman died, just one day short of his 91st birthday on March 16, 2006. Except for his counterintelligence assignment with the U.S. Army in World War II, he had remained officially linked with the university as a coach, volunteer, and chairman of the Georgia Student Educational Fund.

As it turned out, Mehre and Hartman left Georgia at the same time. Mehre would move on to Ole Miss as head coach, and Hartman would leave to play for the Redskins. But his heart remained in Athens, which is why he was eager to join his old GMC coach, Wallace Butts, when Butts became the Bulldog head coach in 1939.

Even in 1938, the year of Joel Hunt, Hartman had lobbied for Butts to become head coach a year earlier than it happened.

(Above) Center Quinton Lumpkin, captain of the 1938 Bulldogs, was known for his ferocity on, and off, the field. He is shown here in the 1950s when he worked for Georgia as a recruiter and assistant coach. (Opposite page) Coach Mehre poses with his coaching staff.

He would complement Butts as backfield coach during the glory days of the 1940s. He would also work with the punters, something that enabled him to return to the practice field as a coach with Vince Dooley in the 1970s and '80s. He was appropriately identified as a "volunteer" coach.

Bill Hartman was always volunteering and serving his alma mater, and was truly one of the giants of Bulldog athletic history.

NEXT: The Little Round Man becomes head coach. The Dawgs at war. UGA's first Rose Bowl.

THE LITTLE ROUND MAN

1938–1963
RECORD: 155 WINS, 106 LOSSES, 14 TIES

Wallace Butts got Georgia into the bowl business—something that the town of Athens passionately longed for but had thus far been denied.

When Harry Mehre left Athens for Ole Miss following the 1937 season, a dogged scramble ensued for the position of head football coach. Eventually a former star player at Texas A&M, Joel Hunt, won out, but he immediately fell into disfavor.

Hunt talked too much, and when he talked, he seemed to rub everybody the wrong way. His abrasive vernacular made him a pariah from the outset.

There was a fortuitous circumstance in the Hunt debacle, however. One of the nation's most successful high school coaches, James Wallace Butts of Male High in Louisville, Kentucky, took a significant pay cut to join the Bulldog staff as an assistant. He coached the ends.

As Hunt became enveloped in an aggravating personality conflict with almost everybody in the community, his popularity plunged so completely that his tenure was terminated after a single season, during which he posted a 5-4-1 record. Not even a 0-0 tie with Georgia Tech could bring him back for another season.

When it was official that Hunt was out, it wasn't long before Butts was in. His reign as head coach would last 22 seasons. There would be four SEC titles on his watch, and the "Little Round Man" would field National Championship teams in 1942 and 1946.

A native Georgian who was elected to the College Football Hall of Fame, Wallace Butts got Georgia into the bowl business—something that the town of Athens passionately longed for but had thus far been denied. Butts' teams won classic games in the Rose Bowl, Orange Bowl, and Sugar Bowl, and he became known as the "Bowlmaster."

He coached 12 All-America players, and two of his pupils—Frank Sinkwich, who won the Heisman trophy, and Charley Trippi, who won the Maxwell Award—became fabled stars whose legends remain prominent in Bulldog history and affectionate lore to this day.

(Preceding page) A 1929 Mercer University graduate, James Wallace "Wally" Butts was UGA's head football coach and athletic director from 1939 to 1963. His determination to win led the Bulldogs to four SEC championships, eight bowl games, and an impressive 140-86-9 record. Known for his dynamic sidelines coaching, he is seen here encouraging his players in a game against Tech during the 1940s.

10 BIG GAMES REMEMBERED: 1938–1963

November 1, 1941: Georgia 7, Auburn 0, at Columbus. This game caused great excitement among the Bulldog fans. The "point-a-minute" Bullpups had come of age. With time running out and no score in the game, Frank Sinkwich threw a 40-yard touchdown pass to Lamar "Racehorse" Davis as the gun sounded. This game provided one of the most dramatic scores in Georgia history and had a lot to do with bringing about the school's first bowl bid. On to Miami!

BULLDOGS

Wallace Butts was a lovable, colorful, and unforgettable character, a humorous and sensitive man who experienced both the high of coaching his team to the National Championship and the low of being accused by a sensational magazine of attempting to fix a Georgia game.

An almost meek and timid man off the field, Butts was driven, dominating, and unrelenting when his practice sessions began.

The toast of the state in the 1940s, Butts developed seven bowl teams in 10 years. The 1950s were lean and harsh until he came back to win his last SEC championship in 1959 with a hometown boy, Francis Asbury Tarkenton. Butts' practices were, in the long-standing football vernacular, forever hard-nosed.

His generosity and his open-house style endeared him and his family to countless alumni and friends. He entertained fans on the field with his passing schemes, and he entertained them off the field with his endless humor and charm. If there were a Raconteur Hall of Fame, Butts would be a charter member. Unfortunately, many who bellied up to his bar in good times would later join the corps of critics.

(Top) Vassa Cate breaks through the Auburn line in 1939.
(Left) Future All-America Frank Sinkwich runs with the ball against Tech in 1939. (Below) In 1941, Sinkwich races for the end zone against Alabama.

GEORGIA COACHES *LIT 1941- Standing-L to R- Lumpkin, Hartman, Lutz, Trainer, Hollis
Kneeling- L to R- Butts, Head Coach, Whitworth, Sikes, Townes, Lampe

10 BIG GAMES REMEMBERED: 1938–1963

January 1, 1942: Georgia 40, Texas Christian University 26, in Miami. Coach Butts had his team primed for peak performance. Led by Frank Sinkwich—who set an Orange Bowl total offensive record of 382 yards—Georgia outclassed the Horned Frogs. Butts would later say that game was the greatest offensive performance of any of his teams. The Bulldogs gained 499 yards total offense on that hot afternoon.

Early in his career, Butts was first and foremost an indefatigable recruiter. As soon as he was hired, he sought players all over the South and as far north as Ohio and Pennsylvania.

In 1939, his first year as the Bulldogs head coach, the team did not fare so well, posting a 5-6 record. But his freshman team, the Bullpups, had all of Athens salivating. Led by Frank Sinkwich, they defeated their three opponents overwhelmingly: South Carolina freshmen, 68-0; Georgia Military College, 65-7; and the Georgia Tech freshmen, 33-0. Georgia Military, the only team to score against this powerhouse, netted three yards rushing.

The next season, 1940, the Bulldogs finished an undistinguished 5-4-1, dampening the spirits of fans who wanted the Bullpups-turned-sophomores to take the team to new heights.

The fans finally got their wish in 1941—only a loss to Alabama in Birmingham and a tie with Harry Mehre's Ole Miss team in Athens, 14-14, kept the Bulldogs from an undefeated season. Moreover, in November, Georgia defeated Tech for the second year in a row. When Butts walked into his suite at the Biltmore Hotel following the game and announced softly that his team had been invited to the Orange Bowl, word soon filtered out into the lobby and subsequently across the state as Georgia fans euphorically celebrated the bowl-invitation breakthrough.

Though the win over Tech was sweet, the game that for the most part had brought about the invitation had taken place against Auburn in Columbus earlier that month. The Bulldogs had defeated the Tigers 7-0 that day, with the most dramatic touchdown in Bulldog history. It also proved to be one of the most important, in that it brought about that first bowl invitation.

The touchdown came about like this: late in the game, Frank Sinkwich, at tailback, faded back and heaved the ball downfield, and wingback Lamar Davis, appropriately nicknamed "Racehorse" because of his remarkable speed, ran under the ball and caught it for the only score of the game. With Sinkwich's pass in the air, the timekeeper's gun sounded. Time had expired when Racehorse gathered in the pass.

Davis' performance that day was no fluke. His big-play-making ability was confirmed year after year by

In 1942, fullback Frank Sinkwich (No. 21, right) welcomed a Pennsylvania native to the team, halfback Charley Trippi (No. 62, left). As a duo the men seemed unbeatable, leading the Bulldogs to a spectacular 11-1 season that culminated in an invitation to the Rose Bowl.

Frank Sinkwich broke his jaw early in the 1941 season. Undaunted, he played the remaining regular season games with a wired jaw and a cumbersome leather protector attached to his helmet. He wore the device at the 1942 Orange Bowl in Miami when the Bulldogs played Texas Christian University, winning 40–26.

his long-distance runs as a receiver and kick-returner: 1939, five TDs; 1940, four TDs; 1941, 13 TDs and one extra point (when the center snapped the ball over the kicker's head, Racehorse, who was the holder, retrieved the ball and weaved his way 30 yards to score the extra point). And finally, in 1942, eight TDs.

His record for average gain per catch (19 for 542 yards, for an average of 28.5 yards) is a mark that could very well stand forever. The fact that he played in the same backfield with Sinkwich and Trippi in 1942 is testament to the genius of Coach Butts, who found a way to integrate the Bulldogs' fleet-footed wingback into his high-powered offense.

As for tailback Frank Sinkwich, his excellent play in that fateful game was made despite a broken jaw, which he'd sustained during the South Carolina game in early October. The tough native of Youngstown,

Ohio, couldn't be kept out of the lineup. He simply came back to play football wearing a protective mask.

An accurate passer and a superb punter, Sinkwich, who'd be elected to the College Football Hall of Fame in 1954, was best described by John Rauch, the quarterback who followed "Flatfoot Frankie" to Georgia. Rauch worked out with Sinkwich in the off-season in Athens, where Sinkwich spent his downtime while playing for the Detroit Lions. Rauch said,

> *His physique didn't look like that of Heisman backs but did give him a unique style. With hips wider than his*

shoulders and short legs, the Fireball looked squat. This build gave him a low center of gravity and enabled him to lean forward as he ran. He could accelerate, stop, and change directions with extreme quickness, thereby eluding tacklers.

Sinkwich went on to complete the 1941 season with his team, and his reputation, already electrifying, soared nationally. He turned in a record-setting performance in Miami, establishing an Orange Bowl record for total offense with 382 yards as the Bulldogs outclassed Texas Christian University from the opening kickoff, 40–26.

The 1942 season turned out to be a big one, both for the team and for Sinkwich, who would lead the Bulldogs to the National Championship and an invitation to the Rose Bowl. He would also win the Heisman Trophy.

The Rose Bowl team was powerful, with depth across the board. Reserve guard Bob Poss, the court jester of the team, always quipped, "I was third team, and I was good."

Van Davis, a rugged end, was one of the most underrated football players in America. George Poschner, the other end, was the consummate competitor. "He had the guts of a burglar," said Bill Hartman. The linemen included Bill Godwin, Bulldog Williams, Harry Kuniansky, Walter Ruark, Gene Ellenson, and

The 1942 National Championship team poses proudly on campus in their distinctive crimson and black letter sweaters.

J.P. Miller. Many were rawboned country boys who felt honored to play for Butts. Their work ethic made them ideal subscribers to Butts' Spartan coaching style.

The Georgia teammates had the time of their lives in Pasadena, socializing with movie stars like Susan Hayward, Ginger Rogers, Ava Gardner, Mickey Rooney, Joe E. Brown, Loretta Young, Kay Kyser, and Bob Hope.

They had fun when the game started, too, although they didn't gain the advantage until the fourth quarter. Red Boyd blocked a punt out of the end zone for a safety, and Charley Trippi enjoyed one of the greatest days of his career by gaining 115 yards rushing. He remains a member of the Helms Foundation's all-time Rose Bowl team.

Sinkwich, hobbled by two sprained ankles, didn't play until the Bulldogs, behind Trippi's fluid rushing efforts, moved downfield late, following a Clyde Ehrhardt interception. Coach Butts sent Sinkwich into the lineup, and he got the ball into the end zone from the UCLA one-yard line for the only touchdown of the game. The score gave Georgia a 9-0 victory.

The team returned home and immediately went off to war. The budding dynasty was halted. No telling what kind of teams Wallace Butts would have produced if Adolf Hitler had stuck to painting.

The excitement that had reached a crescendo in 1942 was reduced to a whisper in 1943 and '44, as everyone focused on a larger event—the culmination of World War II. During that time, the Bulldogs fielded teams composed mostly of 4-Fs and players too young for the draft.

(Right) In 1941, Frank Sinkwich earned All-America honors as UGA's starting tailback.

BULLDOGS®

1938–1963

Charles Trippi grew up in rural Pennsylvania, the son of a Sicilian immigrant coal miner. In 1940, his high school exploits on the gridiron attracted the attention of local Coca-Cola bottler Harold Ketron, a former star of the Bulldog team in 1903. Seeing the boy's potential, Ketron arranged for a scholarship for Trippi to attend the University of Georgia.

Alabama in Birmingham, and the Tide won 28-14. Georgia then rallied to defeat its last four opponents, allowing only seven points to Chattanooga, then shutting out Florida, Auburn, and Georgia Tech.

The 8-2 record resulted in the team's invitation to the Oil Bowl in Houston, where the Bulldogs defeated Tulsa 20-6. Trippi zigzagged his way through the entire Tulsa team on a punt return of 68 yards, a play that for years was labeled the greatest punt return of all time.

And there was more good news: with a year of eligibility left, Trippi passed up all options to turn pro, and planned a return for the 1946 season. In an emotional speech following the Oil Bowl, Butts praised Trippi in the most flattering terms and announced in an unprecedented move that the "Scintillating Sicilian" (as Dan Magill called the Bulldog super-back) would captain the 1946 team. "Coach Butts was almost in tears," recalled John Donaldson, who was slated to take Trippi's place after the coal miner's son from Pittston, Pennsylvania, graduated.

When 1946 arrived, Trippi led the Bulldogs to an undefeated season. The team clinched the National Championship with a 20-10 victory over North Carolina in the Sugar Bowl, in which Trippi outshone fabled Tar Heels back Charlie "Choo-Choo" Justice. During the season, the Bulldogs had scored an average of 37.2 points per game and had allowed an average of 10 points. The closest game was a 14-0 victory over Alabama in Athens, when the Crimson Tide's heralded quarterback, Harry Gilmer, failed to complete a single pass.

Trippi was described by Georgia Tech's Bobby Dodd as the greatest player he'd ever seen. In addition to playing both ways, Trippi was also the team's punter and punt returner. It would take four scholarships today to handle Trippi's responsibilities in 1946.

When 1945 rolled around, excitement began to build again as the players, now soldiers, began coming home from the war. The Bulldogs had gotten off to a good start, defeating their first four teams, when Trippi returned. He was back in time to suit up for the LSU game on October 20. LSU came to Athens and outclassed the Bulldogs 32-0, bursting the team's bubble of high hopes. Trippi was still adjusting to the T-formation the next week, during a face-off against

1938–1963

BULLDOGS

−52−

When Georgia Bulldog Bill Godwin (standing far left) went to Pasadena to play UCLA in the 1942 Rose Bowl, he was thrilled to meet film star Susan Hayward, star of Reap the Wild Wind, then playing in theaters nationwide. Godwin's mother saved this photo in her scrapbook for many years.

It was Harold Ketron who'd sent Trippi to Georgia in the first place. Ketron, the Coca-Cola bottler in Wilkes-Barre, Pennsylvania, kept calling Coach Butts late in the evening after a few shooters, singing Trippi's praises and calling him "the slickest halfback I have ever seen." One night, Coach Butts needled Ketron, asking, "Just how slick is this guy Trippi?" With that, Ketron, a mountain boy from Clarkesville with a thorough knowledge of the woods, drawled, "Wally, he is slicker than owl manure in the moonlight." Except that he used a more graphic word.

Charley Trippi could not stay in college forever. When he left, there was a drop in victory totals, although one of the greatest quarterbacks Butts ever had, John Rauch, was only a junior. He would become the first of two Bulldog quarterbacks (David Greene was the other) to start every game of his varsity career *plus* four bowl games. To the best of my knowledge, Rauch and Greene are the only two players in college football history with that distinction. A debilitating hamstring injury in '46 sidelined Donaldson, who possessed the speed, agility, and accelerating moves that would have made him an ideal left halfback—the key position in the T-formation—when Trippi departed.

The Bulldogs of '47 lost three games by a mere 43 points combined, but with seven victories, they received an invitation to the Gator Bowl. There they tied Maryland, 20-20, when time expired with Georgia on the Terps' goal line.

When Frank Sinkwich won the 1942 Heisman Trophy, he immediately became the idol of thousands of Georgia boys, who dreamed of one day emulating his feats on the college gridiron.

THE HEISMAN MEMORIAL TROPHY
IS PRESENTED BY
DOWNTOWN ATHLETIC CLUB OF NEW YORK CITY
TO
FRANK SINKWICH
UNIVERSITY OF GEORGIA
AS THE
OUTSTANDING COLLEGE FOOTBALL PLAYER
IN THE UNITED STATES
FOR
1942

The 1942 Bulldogs pose on this Pasadena practice field just days before the New Year's Day Rose Bowl game.

---

10 BIG GAMES REMEMBERED:
1938–1963

January 1, 1943: Georgia 9, UCLA 0, Pasadena. For the first three quarters, the Bruins had difficulty containing Charley Trippi, who gained 115 yards without scoring. During the last quarter, guard Red Boyd broke through and blocked a punt out of the end zone to give Georgia a 2–0 lead. That would have been enough for a victory, but after a Clyde Ehrhardt interception, Trippi led the Bulldogs toward the goal. Coach Butts sent in Sinkwich, hobbled by two sprained ankles, to score the only touchdown of the game.

It was championship time again in 1948 when the Bulldogs lost only one regular-season game—to North Carolina. Ken McCall's dazzling 54-yard punt return was the margin of victory in the Tech game. The Dogs were leading 14-7 in a hard-fought match when McCall fielded a Tech punt on the run and hotfooted it into the end zone. On the sideline, Tech's Bobby Dodd, preparing to make a substitution, said to the sub, "That kid just broke up a damn good football game."

Georgia was a heavy favorite when it played Texas in the Orange Bowl following the '48 season. The Longhorns were derided as a "third-rate team" by the press, which repeatedly castigated Orange Bowl

officials for inviting Texas to Miami. Tom Landry was a hard-running fullback for Texas and was the big star of the game, which Texas won 41-28.

"They were ready, and we were not," remembered Dick Yelvington, a young tackle who would become Landry's teammate with the New York Giants. "What I remember is their band constantly playing 'The Eyes of Texas Are Upon You.' That damn band played so loud and hard and often. I can remember that we felt like it gave their team a big lift," Yelvington said.

BULLDOGS

OIL BOWL 1946

When Charley Trippi, left, was discharged from the Air Force after World War II he returned to UGA for the final six games of 1945, including the Oil Bowl in Houston against Tulsa. The Bulldogs won 20-6.

By 1946, female cheerleaders were becoming a common sight on college campuses nationwide.

In 1945, Georgia beat Auburn a whopping 35-0. The Bulldogs' Alabama rival put up a fight, however, as this Auburn Tiger tries to forcibly "relieve" quarterback John Donaldson of his leather helmet. Donaldson later became a backfield coach under Vince Dooley.

The 1949 season was not a successful one, giving Butts his first losing season (4-6-1) since his initial year as head coach. The toughest loss of the season was at Georgia Tech. The Jackets won 7-6, beginning a long and hideous winning streak that was to embitter Bulldogs fans. It would be eight years before the Red and Black banner would wave victoriously on the Saturday after Thanksgiving.

The 1950 team (6-2-3 in the regular season) gave up only 65 points, a record for an 11-game schedule. Georgia could not score enough points when it counted, though, and lost all the close games, including the finale to Georgia Tech, 7-0, in Athens. The Bulldogs were invited to the Presidential Cup at College Park, Maryland, where they lost 40-20 to Texas A&M. It would be nine long years before another bowl invitation would come about.

The 1952 team (7-4) and the team of 1954 (6-3-1) were the only winning teams from 1951 to 1959. Naturally, there was a gnashing of teeth among the Bulldog faithful. The frustration of falling on hard times was further exacerbated by the annual loss to Tech.

Butts had banked so much goodwill with his teams in the '40s that he survived amid rancor and contempt. Much of his ability to weather the storm had to do with the fact that he had always expressed an undying love for the University of Georgia.

(Above) In 1948, end Bob Walston led the SEC in receiving, and was voted All-SEC the following year. In 1951, he earned NFL Rookie of the Year with the Philadelphia Eagles.

10 BIG GAMES REMEMBERED: 1938–1963

November 2, 1946: Georgia 14, Alabama 0, at Athens. This game received considerable hype, as it matched up Georgia's Charley Trippi with Alabama's Harry Gilmer. Trippi easily took control as the star of the game. On Georgia's end of the field, his punt was blocked and a mad scramble ensued for the ball. Even though a couple of Alabama players had the advantage in regard to proximity, it was Trippi who dove into the pileup and came up with the ball. Gilmer, a fine player who would go on to great success in the NFL, did not complete a single pass that day.

January 1, 1947: Georgia 20, North Carolina 10, in New Orleans. Charley Trippi's last game as a Bulldog was a classic. The Tar Heels were coached by Carl Snavely and led by Charlie "Choo Choo" Justice. In this battle of the Charlies, Trippi was the victor. Coach Butts had the distinction of never having lost a bowl game, and at no time were the Bulldogs playing the Little Sisters of the Poor. The post-game celebration was tempered with the awareness that Trippi had put on his Georgia No. 62 jersey for the last time.

Georgia was playing to small crowds, the athletic coffers were pretty much empty, and nothing seemed to go right for the man who'd been the toast of the state in the '40s.

Then, *finally* . . . on November 30, 1957, his fortunes took an upswing. It was a cold and windy day on Grant Field, and Theron Sapp was playing fullback. A square-jawed, crew-cut young man, he'd overcome a broken neck in high school to continue in football—giving rise to this question: has anybody ever wanted to play football for the Bulldogs more than the "Macon

Charley Trippi and Coach Wally Butts hand out toys to Athens children at the Salvation Army on Christmas Eve, 1947.

Mauler"? Sapp blasted through the Tech defense on fourth down to score the only touchdown of the day. Hallelujah, the Dogs were on top in the ancient rivalry once again!

The drought had been broken, and the state has never had a greater hero for a day than Theron Sapp. Appreciative as always, Sapp was eager to share praise with his teammates—the rock-jawed defense, the blocking by the offensive line on his touchdown plunge. "And don't forget Jimmy Orr," he said. "He caught a third-down pass of 13 yards to keep the drive alive."

So grateful were the Bulldog fans that a move to retire Sapp's jersey met with emotional success. While his credentials are no match for those established by the three other jersey retirees (Frank Sinkwich, Charley Trippi, and Herschel Walker), it is not lost on him why his number, 40, was retired. "My jersey," he said with the greatest of humility, "was retired by the Georgia people."

A year later, the Bulldogs lacked consistent offensive punch against Alabama, Florida, and Auburn, and lost six games but defeated Tech for the second year in a row, 16-3.

In early 1959, good news surfaced for Georgia with the announcement that J.B. Whitworth, the line coach in Butts' heyday of the '40s, would return in that same capacity to the Bulldogs.

Led by Fran Tarkenton and Pat Dye, with an offensive assist from Charley Britt on a 39-yard punt return for a touchdown, Georgia defeated Auburn 14-13 to claim the Southeastern Conference championship—Butts' fourth.

It was the heroics of Dye and Tarkenton that brought about the victory late in the game. Auburn was leading 13-7 with less than three minutes to play in the game. Quarterback Bryant Harvard, from Thomasville, Georgia, fumbled (thanks to Bulldog Bill Herron), and Pat Dye, quick and decisive, recovered the ball to set the stage for a last-ditch opportunity.

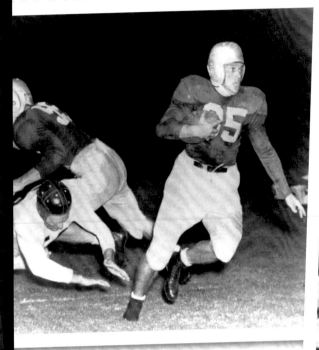

(Above) Halfback Joe Geri (No. 35) was drafted in the fourth round of the 1949 NFL draft by the Pittsburgh Steelers. He later played for the Chicago Cardinals before being inducted into the Georgia Sports Hall of Fame. (Right) Fullback Theron Sapp (40) on the run in 1958's 78-0 victory over the Citadel. Sapp said his "jersey was retired by the Georgia people"

10 BIG GAMES REMEMBERED: 1938–1963

November 27, 1948: Georgia 21, Georgia Tech 13, at Athens. The Bulldogs of 1948 brought Coach Butts his third SEC title of the 1940s. Led by senior John Rauch, the Bulldogs would win the championship, and they expected an invitation back to the Orange Bowl if they beat Georgia Tech in the finale in Athens. Tech would not go quietly as they had in 1942 and 1946. The Bulldogs were leading 14–7 late in the game when lightning struck: Ken McCall, with sprinter's speed, fielded a Yellow Jacket punt on the run and raced 54 yards for a decisive touchdown, which would put the game out of reach. On the sideline, Tech's Bobby Dodd said, "That kid just broke up a damn good football game."

Dye, a two-time All-American for the Bulldogs, was always around the ball. His list of big plays was numerous and consequential, as he was one of the special players who helped lead Coach Butts back to prominence. He stole the ball against Kentucky on a kickoff one year and returned it for a touchdown. He also tipped the pass that Charley Britt returned for 100 yards in the 1959 Florida game, among other big plays. But the plays that exemplified Dye's exceptional skills and unparalleled play-making competitiveness came in the Tech game his senior year. He blocked an extra point and a field-goal attempt, which was the margin of victory in a 7–6 game.

So when the ball came loose against Auburn, anybody who knew Pat Dye would have bet he would be the man to claim the bouncing pigskin.

Now it was Tarkenton's turn. Starting at the Auburn 35-yard line, Tarkenton moved the Bulldogs goalward, completing the drive with a fourth down and a 13-yard touchdown pass to Bill Herron. The key plays were passes over the middle to Don Soberdash, a compact, quick, and energized fullback who had just returned to the lineup after being hobbled with a bad knee. Following Durward Pennington's extra point, the Bulldogs were SEC champions, 14–13.

Tarkenton exhibited skills in his last two seasons that were to accommodate him famously in the National Football League. On the touchdown pass to Herron, he drew up the play in the grass at the east end of Sanford Stadium.

He directed Herron to block and count, "one thousand and one, one thousand and two, one thousand and three." Then, Herron was instructed to release and run a down-and-out pattern to the corner of the end zone. In the meantime, Tarkenton had rolled to his right, drawing the Auburn defense to that side of the field. He pulled up and calmly threw the ball back across the field to a wide-open Herron. In those days, it was rare for a quarterback to roll to his right and throw back across his body to his left. Tarkenton's long and distinguished NFL career confirmed that he was inventive, creative, and exceptional.

Unfortunately for him, the one-platoon-substitution rules of that era inhibited in large part his consummate quarterback skills. Throughout his long career in the NFL, Tarkenton called his plays and worked with all his coaches to effect a short-game passing attack that resulted in these NFL career records: most passing attempts, 6,467; most pass completions, 3,686; most yards passing, 47,003; and most touchdown passes, 342.

While he learned the importance of remaining in the pocket—an unyielding dictum of his head coach—Tarkenton would scramble to make a play when the protection broke down. It was the art of buying time, which became a staple of his play early in his professional career.

In the spring of 1960, the Bulldogs suffered a depressing blow when beloved line coach J.B. Whitworth suffered a heart attack and died. Whitworth is widely given credit for bringing about the best of morale and motivation for the Bulldogs of 1959.

(From top to bottom) Zeke Bratkowski (No. 12), Theron Sapp (No. 40), and Charley Britt (No. 17) were some of UGA's most recognized players of the 1950s.

In 1950, assistant coaches Ralph "Shug" Jordan, Bill Hartman, and Sterling DuPree relax in the Georgia locker room with Coach Butts and his dog Rip. The following year, Jordan left for his alma mater, Auburn University, to take over its lagging football program.

Not only did he bring years of coaching experience back to Athens, where he and Butts, along with Bill Hartman, were regarded as an unbeatable team in the 1940s; the players gravitated to Whitworth and his colossal charm. He was tough and not only preached, but demanded, discipline. However, he reached out with a grandfatherly, inspirational touch to the entire team. B-team player Paul Holmes said years later, "He made us feel part of the team. He told us we couldn't have won the SEC title and gotten to the Orange Bowl if the B-team hadn't tested the varsity in practice to where they were always ready to play on Saturday."

In 1960, Tarkenton and Dye were seniors, and Coach Butts' last captains. Georgia lost four games: Alabama at Birmingham, 21-6; Southern Cal at Los Angeles, 10-3; Florida at Jacksonville, 22-14; and Auburn at Auburn, 9-6—two field goals to three. A victory at Auburn would surely have sent Butts into retirement with a bowl invitation.

Early in 1961, talk began to spread that Butts would be giving up coaching at Georgia. Many rumors had developed about off-the-field conflicts, but it still came as a shock to most when Butts suddenly announced his retirement on January 6, 1961.

(Above) Fran Tarkenton (No. 10) is considered by many to be one of football's best quarterbacks. When he graduated from UGA in 1960, he embarked upon a pro career spanning 18 years. (Left) Tarkenton, left, and Pat Dye, right, pose with coach Wally Butts in 1960.

10 BIG GAMES REMEMBERED: 1938–1963

November 30, 1957: Georgia 7, Georgia Tech 0, at Atlanta. The 1950s were not good to Wallace Butts, as his teams were not the fabled squads he had fielded in the heyday of the '40s. But a new day dawned for Butts and his downtrodden Bulldogs on Grant Field on this day. It was like an arm-wrestling contest, with neither team gaining the advantage. Finally, in the fourth quarter, Georgia mounted a drive that ended with a touchdown by Theron Sapp, giving the Bulldogs a 7-0 victory. So grateful were the fans for beating Tech, there was a move to retire Sapp's No. 40 jersey. The effort succeeded.

He would stay on as athletic director, but he put down his coaching whistle with the knowledge that he had finished on top—another SEC title and major bowl bid, and the distinction of defeating the archenemy, Georgia Tech, four years in a row.

It was not a smooth exit, however. Johnny Griffith, who had played and coached for the Little Round Man and was the Bulldogs' chief recruiter, succeeded Butts. Unfortunately, there was little harmony in Athens.

It was apparent that Butts was not happy in his exclusively administrative job, and there never was any rapport between him and Griffith. Most of Butts' friends felt he preferred to be on the field teaching his vaunted passing attack.

The year 1963 was Griffith's third, and what turned out to be his final, season. His teams had trouble winning close games, tying four games in two seasons. There was bickering and dissention all around. Griffith, a good man, never really had a chance.

In March 1963, news broke that the *Saturday Evening Post* would be publishing a story accusing Butts and Alabama's Bear Bryant of trying to fix the 1962 Georgia-Alabama game. Butts resigned his athletic directorship a broken man.

Butts went on television before the magazine's accusation hit the streets and categorically denied the story. A federal jury in Atlanta in August 1963 vindicated Butts with a $3,060,000 judgment, which was subsequently reduced by the judge to $460,000. But the amount didn't matter—his worst nightmare had ended.

He became a successful insurance salesman and a popular after-dinner speaker, but his golden years were all too brief. On December 17, 1973, he died of a heart attack following a winter's jog in the streets near his home.

(Above) Johnny Griffith, on left with assistant coach Wyatt Posey, was the coach of the freshman squad under Butts and succeeded Butts as UGA head coach.

10 BIG GAMES REMEMBERED: 1938–1963

November 14, 1959: Georgia 14, Auburn 13, at Athens. Auburn arrived for a game Between the Hedges, the first time since 1916 that the game had not been played in Columbus. With the visitors leading 13-7 and less than three minutes left to play, Auburn's Bryant Harvard fumbled (recovery by who else but Pat Dye), and Tarkenton's troops took over at the War Eagle 35-yard line. At fourth down and with only seconds left on the clock, Tarkenton drew up a play in the huddle and calmly passed to Bill Herron for the touchdown. Durward Pennington's extra point gave Butts one of his sweetest victories, 14-13.

The 1959 Bulldogs board a plane to Miami to take on Missouri at the Orange Bowl.

NEXT: Dooley takes over. 1968's special players. Bringing SEC titles to Athens. The Herschel Walker Era. Winning the National Championship.

BULLDOGS

1938-1963

How 'Bout Them Dawgs?

1964–1988
Record: 201 wins, 80 losses, 10 ties

The Dooley era was Georgia's greatest. Garnering a National Championship and six SEC titles, Dooley ball was winning ball.

Vince Dooley arrived in Athens a little-known freshman coach from Auburn. At 31, he was one of the Bulldogs' youngest head coaches. He would finish his coaching career as Georgia's winningest coach.

Dooley and Joel Eaves, the athletic director who hired him, kept to themselves at the outset. That didn't sit well with Wally Butts loyalists in the community. Dooley could be perceived as distant and aloof, whereas Butts was a charming raconteur. Dooley ball, while eminently successful—six SEC titles and a National Championship—was the antithesis of the passing game of Wally's boys. Dooley ball, more often than not, offered a safe and secure route to victory: run the ball, play proficient defense, and employ sound kicking principles. Don't beat yourself. Fans often grumbled about Dooley's air of stiffness or his three-yards-and-a-cloud-of-dust offense. Right out of the box, however, his first team won seven games, defeated Georgia Tech for the first time in four years, and was invited to play in the Sun Bowl at El Paso, where the upstart Bulldogs defeated Texas Tech 7-0. It was a prelude to greater things.

Born during the Depression, young Vince learned about life in the streets, and this experience taught him about competition, survival, and how to stay the course. He was a quick and eager learner and developed an inner toughness from which he benefited constantly during his accomplished career.

His mother often reminded him that "manners will take you where money won't," and his father underscored the idea that "a commitment is a commitment." Add to this a strict Catholic upbringing, which consistently emphasized discipline, scholarship, and responsibility, and you have the background and training for success, self-improvement, and achievement—provided a kid had even the slightest motivation. In those days, hard times were not necessarily bad times.

When he went to Auburn to play football on scholarship, Vince looked forward to the excitement of collegiate competition. He was anxious to learn whether he could compete on a higher level.

(Preceding page) Georgia head coach Vince Dooley goes over the top of his players to receive congratulations from Alabama's Paul "Bear" Bryant after the upstart Bulldogs surprised the defending national champs 18-17 in 1965, Dooley's second season at UGA. (Above) Dooley rolled into Athens from Auburn in 1964, but Georgia fans were quickly captivated by the new regime.

After taking over the Bulldogs, Dooley's 1964 team beat Kentucky 21-7 (above) but lost to Alabama 31-3 (below) during a successful first season at UGA.

At Auburn, Vince played football and basketball, and was a starter in both sports. When he heard rumors that some of the athletes were getting a little more than their basic scholarship's worth, he complained to a Mobile banker who had helped recruit him to Auburn.

"In my flawed thinking," Dooley recalled, "I thought that since I was starting in two sports, I was worth two scholarships." The banker pointed out that in return for Vince's athletic efforts, his scholarship offered him a free education—no more, no less. It was never an issue after that—Vince Dooley gave Auburn his best on the field and in the classroom.

Winning always made Dooley's personality more agreeable. Early in his coaching career, I complained that he needed to be more outgoing, and he always replied, "A man can't change his personality." Those who have known him from his beginning days will tell you that he has, in fact, changed. Today he is damn near a reincarnation of Dale Carnegie.

After that encouraging seven-win start in 1964, Dooley's second season was more up-and-down, but Georgia's ragtag boys played with the hearts of lions.

The new regime captivated the town of Athens from the start.

The opening game pitted Dooley and the upstart Bulldogs against the defending national champions and their grizzled veteran coach, Bear Bryant. Big plays were the order of the day for Georgia. Early in the game, Georgia tackle Jiggy Smaha slammed into quarterback Steve Sloan, who was about to release a pass. The ball fluttered into the air, and defensive tackle George Patton, a one-time quarterback, gathered in the ball and raced 55 yards for a touchdown.

Alabama, playing efficiently and flawlessly, took the lead and was ahead 17–10 late in the fourth quarter when Dooley sent word to quarterback Kirby Moore to run the flea flicker, a play that had never seemed to work in practice.

This was one time, however, that it worked perfectly. Moore dropped back and threw a low pass to the button-hooking Pat Hodgson, who shoveled it to Bob Taylor, who was sprinting by as planned. Alabama's defense, efficiently schooled by Bryant in the art of gang-tackling, converged on Hodgson en masse, and Taylor raced 73 yards for the touchdown.

Some of Dooley's 1964 Bulldogs on the practice field. They are (from left to right) defensive back Mark Holmes, linebacker Steve Nieuhaus, defensive back Terry Sellers, and quarterback Lynn Hughes.

Moore calmly threw the two-point conversion pass to Hodgson. The play brought about a signature victory early in Dooley's tenure. There would be other great plays during his Hall of Fame career, but none more spectacular—except, perhaps, for the pass from Buck Belue to Lindsay Scott in Jacksonville, but that would be a decade and a half later.

Vanderbilt was the next victim of Dooley ball, at 24-10 in Athens. The Bulldogs then traveled to Ann Arbor to battle the defending Rose Bowl champions. The entire campus treated the game as a breather in spite of the Bulldogs' opening-game upset of Alabama.

Erk Russell's defense never played more tenaciously, and quarterback Preston Ridlehuber showed the Big Ten boys something, running the football with a hard-nosed effect that took it to any defender who came up to meet him. With their 15-7 victory, the Bulldogs experienced a homecoming to surpass all homecomings. When the two Southern Airways Martin 404s that were bringing the team home began their descent at the Athens airport, the team and coaches, looking out the windows, were overwhelmed by the multitude of waiting fans. It appeared that all of Athens had tried to make its way to the airport. The car headlights stretched several miles.

There hadn't been such rejoicing since Chancellorsville—and unfortunately, just as Robert E. Lee lost the able Stonewall Jackson in that epic battle, the Bulldogs soon were losing soldiers of their own. One front-line player after another fell to injury. First it was Bob Taylor—pound for pound, one of the toughest running backs ever to wear the Red and Black. Then it was Doug McFalls, Kirby Moore, and Joe Burson. Soon the rest of the team was hobbled, most significantly Preston Ridlehuber, the rugged quarterback.

In the five games from the second week in October through Thanksgiving, only one team went to the Dogs—North Carolina, 47–35, at Chapel Hill. There would be no bowl invitation.

The Bulldogs found some cheer for the holidays, though, when Georgia, with an unbalanced line, went on to surprise Tech 17-7 on Grant Field. This was the game where the enduring and popular phrase "G.A.T.A." was born. At the half, Georgia was leading 10-0. Erk Russell, ever the motivator and slogan entrepreneur, spotted the letters GTAA (for Georgia Tech Athletic Association) stenciled on equipment in the visitors' dressing room.

"Men," he exhorted his players, "let's move one of those A's over by the G and make it G.A.T.A.—Get After Tech's Anatomy" (except Erk used a more graphic concluding word). Erk's motivation worked, and the team had a two-for-two box score in the biggest game on the Bulldog schedule.

While the injury-riddled Dogs struggled, good news was emanating from freshman competition. In his first season, Dooley had enjoyed a banner recruiting year, and the 1965 Bullpups, biding their time for varsity competition, would help bring an SEC Championship to Athens when they became sophomores in 1966.

But before the splendid sophomores could strut their stuff, Oklahoma tried to lure Dooley to Norman with a financial package that turned heads.

During the Georgia–Alabama game back in September, Bud Wilkinson, the Sooner legend who was the color announcer for the NBC telecast, had been impressed with the cool and calm demeanor he'd observed in the young Bulldog coach.

Wilkinson had moved down to the sidelines from the press box for a post-game interview. He was standing near Dooley following the flea-flicker touchdown, and when the 32-year-old coach nodded in

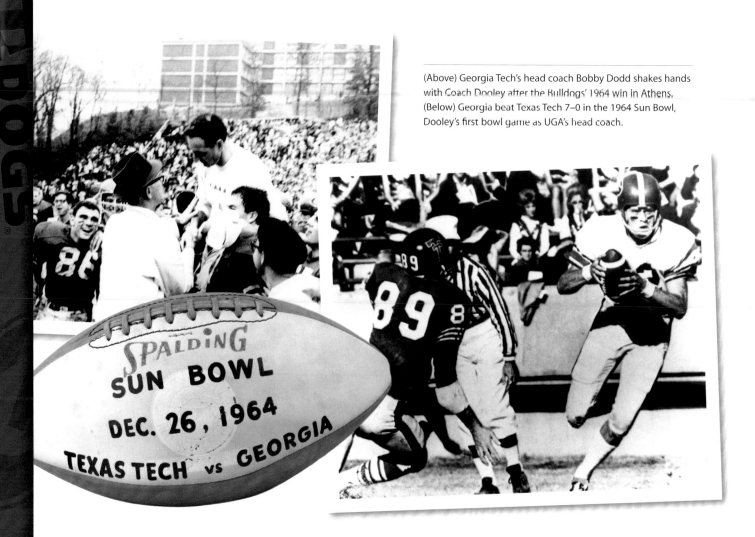

(Above) Georgia Tech's head coach Bobby Dodd shakes hands with Coach Dooley after the Bulldogs' 1964 win in Athens. (Below) Georgia beat Texas Tech 7–0 in the 1964 Sun Bowl, Dooley's first bowl game as UGA's head coach.

SPALDING
SUN BOWL
DEC. 26, 1964
TEXAS TECH vs GEORGIA

> **10 BIG GAMES REMEMBERED:**
> **1964–1988**
>
> **September 18, 1965:** Georgia 18, Alabama 17, at Athens. With Alabama leading 17–10 late in the game, Georgia needed a big play. The flea flicker had never worked in practice, but Kirby Moore threw to end Pat Hodgson, who flipped the ball to running back Bob Taylor to complete a 73-yard score. A two-point conversion, Moore to Hodgson, gave Dooley a signature victory in only his second season.

his direction and said, "We're going for two!" Wilkinson grinned wildly. Caught up in the excitement of the flea flicker and impressed with the young coach's courage and cool-under-fire temperament, Wilkinson responded, "Yes, we've got to."

Later, when Oklahoma was searching for a new coach, Wilkinson told Sooner officials that the best young coach in the country resided in Athens, Georgia.

Thus a series of negotiations that would impact Georgia's athletic future took place in December of 1965. When Georgia began to devise a counteroffer, Bill Hartman stepped forward with Georgia Student Educational Fund (GSEF) resources and placed a call to tax lawyer M.E. "Buster" Kilpatrick. A former Bulldog quarterback, Kilpatrick designed a financial package that made Georgia's offer more attractive than Oklahoma's.

Barbara Dooley didn't really want to leave Athens, but she and Vince were touched by the fans' pleas to remain. Elmo Ellis of WSB radio in Atlanta even wrote lyrics to the tune of "Hang Down Your Head Tom Dooley," begging the young coach not to leave the University of Georgia.

Dooley had originally taken the Georgia job for $12,000 a year, and he now wanted to be better compensated. He also wanted to be in charge of decisions that would affect the university's football program. Athletic director Joe Eaves acquiesced to his requests, offering him the assistant athletic director position, and that—combined with the new compensation package—persuaded Dooley to stay.

> **10 BIG GAMES REMEMBERED:**
> **1964–1988**
>
> **October 2, 1965:** Georgia 15, Michigan 7, at Ann Arbor. Two weeks after "flea flickering" Alabama, the Bulldogs upset the defending Rose Bowl champions. When the Dogs returned to Athens, it appeared that the entire town had made its way to the airport to sing "Hail to the Victors." No other Georgia team has ever returned home from victory to a celebration matching that one.

(Filmstrip) Late in the fourth quarter against Alabama in 1965, the Bulldogs worked the flea flicker to perfection to beat the defending national champs 18-17 in Athens. It was the Crimson Tide's only loss of the season.

(Top) Coach Dooley receives congratulations from Coach Dodd after the Bulldogs beat Tech 23-14 in 1966. (Above) Dooley visits with members of his varsity squad in 1966 in newly constructed McWhorter Hall, named after Georgia's first All-America player, Bob McWhorter.

The young freshmen of 1965 were now sophomores and ready for varsity action. Bill Stanfill, Jake Scott, Kent Lawrence, Happy Dicks, and Billy Payne, among others, joined veterans like Tommy Lawhorne, Edgar Chandler, and George Patton. Their blend of experience and youth soon led to superb performance between the hedges. The highlights of their season were a 23-14 victory over undefeated Tech in Athens and a 24-9 romp over SMU in the Cotton Bowl. Only a one-point loss to Miami marred the otherwise perfect season.

The team went on to finish 7-3 in 1967, earning an invitation to the Liberty Bowl. And then, in 1968, it was championship time again in Athens. Those freshmen of 1965 had become seniors. Jake Scott and Bill Stanfill led a big-play defense that yielded points grudgingly. Sophomore Mike Cavan was a levelheaded quarterback who displayed the leadership of a seasoned veteran.

The opener in Knoxville was a thriller, with Jake Scott displaying skills that made network color announcer Bud Wilkinson rave throughout the broadcast. Scott made a one-handed stab of an interception that caused the fans to buzz with head-shaking amazement and made Wilkinson practically leap out of his seat. Then, in the second half, Scott had an 80-yard punt return that was as beautiful as any since Charley Trippi. Scott was a slashing runner in the open field and seemed to have just enough speed to outrun any pursuer. Old-timers who'd been around in the 1940s labeled Scott the best safety man since Trippi's day.

They were a special group of players. Not only were they skilled and athletic, they were high achievers and inspirational leaders who would distinguish themselves in their chosen professions after graduation.

Happy Dicks became a neurosurgeon. Billy Payne became a successful lawyer who brought the 1996 Olympics to Atlanta. He also served as the CEO, and chairman, of the Augusta National Golf Club.

Tommy Lawhorne, the valedictorian of his senior class, went on to become a surgeon following graduation from Johns Hopkins, and settled in Columbus, Georgia. Tommy Lyons and Billy Darby also became doctors. Wayne Byrd and Ed Allen became lawyers, and Kent Lawrence is now a judge.

November 12, 1966: Georgia 21, Auburn 13, at Auburn. Vince Dooley's first SEC title came at Auburn, where he had both played and coached. Down 13-0 at the half, the Bulldogs came back with a dominating performance in the final 30 minutes to capture victory, 21-13. This would be the first of six conference championships for Dooley.

Dooley and Bryant chat at a Southeastern Conference meeting in the early 1960s, perhaps discussing the quality of the oysters being served at the event.

BULLDOGS

1964–1988

BULLDOGS

(Above) In 1967, an upper deck of seats was appended to each side of Sanford Stadium, in addition to a new press box and club seating. The 19,640 new seats brought the stadium's capacity to 59,000. (Below) Quarterback Kirby Moore (No. 14) unleashes a sideline pass against SMU in the 1966 Cotton Bowl, which the Bulldogs won 24-9.

Bill Stanfill and Jake Scott became stars with the Miami Dolphins, and their NFL accomplishments equaled those of their remarkable Georgia careers. Scott, in Super Bowl VII, became the first of three former Bulldogs to be named the most valuable player in the NFL title game.

With all that talent graduated, 1969 was a forgettable season. In the last five games, the Bulldogs managed only a tie with Florida, losing four times. Tech won 6-0 in Atlanta, and Nebraska embarrassed the Dogs in the Sun Bowl 45-6. The break-even season, 5-5-l, would be followed by another break-even season, 5-5, in 1970. Tech won for the second year in a row.

Another talented freshman was waiting in the wings, however. In 1971, quarterback Andy Johnson would lead the Bulldogs to a one-loss season and a Gator Bowl victory, 7-0, over North Carolina, a game that featured a coaching match-up of the Dooley brothers. There was so little excitement in the low-scoring contest that sportswriter and Georgia graduate Rex Edmundson quipped, "Vince won the toss and ran the clock out."

During the regular season, however, there were plenty of fireworks. Except for Tulane (17-7) and North Carolina in the Gator Bowl, Georgia scored 20 or more points on every team on the schedule.

The only loss came when Pat Sullivan and Terry Beasley of Auburn had career games between the hedges, spoiling Georgia's championship dreams 35-20.

Chuck Heard (No. 91), Larry Brasher (No. 76) and the rest of the Bulldog defense shut out Tulane 35-0 in the 1969 season opener.

(Above) Despite a valiant effort, the Bulldogs lost the 1969 Sugar Bowl to Arkansas 16-2. (Below) Soon into his UGA coaching career, Dooley redesigned the team's old helmet, branding it with the familiar black "G" worn by players today.

"I've never played harder and got less results," said defensive lineman Chuck Heard. His running mate, Mixon Robinson, exclaimed, "I can't tell you how many times we were a half step away from sacking Sullivan." This game won the Heisman for Sullivan.

Robinson was to experience a perplexing scene two weeks later, following the Tech game in Atlanta. In a hard-fought battle on Thanksgiving night, before a national television audience, Andy Johnson, with 1:29 on the clock, moved the Bulldogs 65 yards downfield to victory, 28-24, with Jimmy Poulos diving over the top for the winning score.

In the jubilation that followed on the field, Robinson was slapping everybody on the back, including his brother Donny, who played for Tech. "Isn't this great?" Mixon exclaimed.

November 25, 1971: Georgia 28, Georgia Tech 24, at Atlanta. With 1:29 left on the clock, quarterback Andy Johnson directed a 65-yard scoring drive with Jimmy Poulas going over the top for a touchdown at the Tech goal line. The Bulldogs had come from behind for one of their greatest victories over the big rival. ABC's network cameras were there, which heightened the celebration.

"Well, no, not really," his brother replied, much to Mixon's chagrin.

Except for '71, '75, '76, and '78, the 1970s were years of mediocrity. The ignominy of losing to Tech's wishbone in the rain and mud in Athens in 1974 was trumped by defeat in the Tangerine Bowl by Miami of Ohio, 21-10. The natives were restless. So restless, in fact, they were calling for Dooley's head.

University president Fred Davison, a big fan who cheered robustly at every Bulldog success, shut all the critics up in late summer when he renewed Dooley's contract for four more years. With one year left on his contract, Dooley had pointed out to Davison that, given the success of the program to date—including two SEC titles—it would be unfair to the staff and the program for him to work under a one-year contract, which would also cause negative media speculation. The two men would develop issues later on with regard to the athletic directorship, but seldom in college-football history has a president stood up for his football coach as Davison did for Dooley in preseason 1975.

Dooley and the rejuvenated Dogs rewarded Davison and the Bulldog Nation with a 9-2 season. Although Georgia lost to Arkansas in the Cotton Bowl, Bulldog fans consoled themselves during the winter months with photos of the Tech scoreboard, taken when Georgia was leading 42-0 in the third quarter.

(Top right) Running back Horace King was UGA's first black football player. King is seen here going "over the top" at the 1973 game against Auburn in Athens. In 1975, he was drafted into the NFL by the Detroit Lions. (Right) "Gliding" Glynn Harrison carries the ball into the end zone during the 1973 Auburn game. The Bulldogs beat the Tigers 28–14 that day.

BULLDOGS

1964–1988

"That is when Coach Dooley magnanimously called off the Dawgs," said Dan Magill—who, after suffering through the drought, celebrated famously any victory over "the enemy."

With quarterback Ray Goff running the veer option to perfection in 1976, Dooley claimed his third SEC title. The Bulldogs averaged 29.4 points per game and gave up an average of 10.7, shutting out four teams. It was Dooley ball at its finest.

By this time, the Junkyard Dawg defense of coach Erk Russell was firmly established. Erk came up with the nickname in 1978, and cartoonist and Bulldog alumnus Jack Davis, who'd produced 36 *Time* covers, created a cartoon drawing of the Junkyard Dawgs that adorned billboards across the state.

Then it was back to a subpar season in 1979. Things became even bleaker in the off-season when the football team, which hosted an annual party known as the Seagraves party, got caught stealing a pig from the university's experimental farm for barbecue purposes.

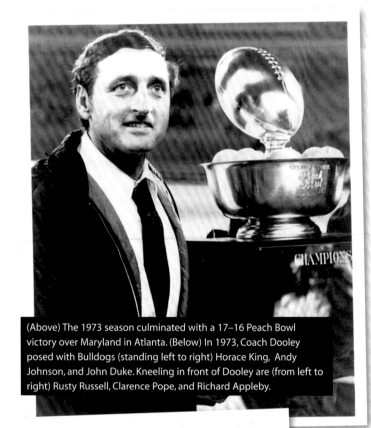

(Above) The 1973 season culminated with a 17–16 Peach Bowl victory over Maryland in Atlanta. (Below) In 1973, Coach Dooley posed with Bulldogs (standing left to right) Horace King, Andy Johnson, and John Duke. Kneeling in front of Dooley are (from left to right) Rusty Russell, Clarence Pope, and Richard Appleby.

GO GEORGIA! 76
JUNKYARD DOGS ARE BACK

In 1974, UGA beat Vanderbilt 38-31, but losses to Georgia Tech and to Miami of Ohio in a bowl game made the natives restless. However, the "Junkyard Dogs" were about to return to dominance.

This episode became one of Dooley's most trying. He was forced to discipline the heart of his football team. Frank Ros, Chris Welton, Nat Hudson, Scott Woerner, and Hugh Nall were soon to be seen painting the concrete fence around the practice field—embarrassing and laborious punishment during one of the hottest summers on record. When they were nearly finished, Dooley came out for an inspection. "It needs another coat," he announced to his crestfallen players, and left.

Much has been written since then about the bonding that took place during this incident. The players agreed that it had a lot to do with the Bulldogs' coming from nowhere to win the National Championship in 1980.

In preseason polls, the writers who covered the SEC teams had ranked Georgia at the bottom. The schedule featured Tennessee, Clemson, South Carolina, Florida, and Auburn—all expected to enjoy better seasons than the Bulldogs.

10 BIG GAMES REMEMBERED: 1964–1988

October 2, 1976: Georgia 21, Alabama 0, at Athens. This was the first time a Bear Bryant team had been shut out in 70 games, an event that touched off a celebration lasting through the weekend and into the next week. Classes were canceled as the Georgia students became so excited that they didn't want to stop the party—and they didn't until mid-week. This ranks as the greatest post-game celebration in memory.

(Above) Erskine "Erk" Russell, pictured here in 1976 with two players, was the Bulldogs' beloved defensive coordinator under Coach Dooley from 1964 to 1981. He later served as head coach for the Georgia Southern Eagles.

The good news, however, was that the Bulldogs had signed Herschel Walker, the sensational back out of Wrightsville, Georgia.

Walker and his capable teammates brought about Dooley's greatest era—three SEC titles, a National Championship, and a record of 33-3. From 1980 to 1981, Georgia lost only one regular-season game: to Clemson in '81, when the Dawgs turned the ball over nine times to lose 13-3. In '82, the Dawgs posted a 10-1-1 record, defeating Texas 10-9 in the Cotton Bowl. The win-loss total for Walker's class, from 1980 to 1983, was a sparkling 43-4-1—the best four-year period ever for the University of Georgia, and the best in the nation at that time.

None of the preseason reports from Athens had forecast that Walker would be dominant as a freshman. Most observers felt that he wouldn't be able to run over linebackers as he had in Class A competition. In fact, he didn't start his first Georgia game, against Tennessee—but once he got into the lineup in the second quarter, he was the big star of the evening. He ran over everybody in orange to score two touchdowns in the second half, as the Bulldogs came from behind (15-0) to emerge victorious, 16-15. When the game was over, he had convinced everybody, including a once-skeptical Dooley, that he was ready to take on all comers in the toughest football conference in the land.

10 BIG GAMES REMEMBERED: 1964–1988

December 2, 1978: Georgia 29, Tech 28, at Athens. Down 28–21 late in the game, the Bulldogs were faced with a fourth-down situation near midfield. Buck Belue hit Anthony Arnold on a 43-yard pass that was followed by a two-point conversion (the end-around handoff to Arnold) and victory. On the TD pass, Arnold, nicknamed "Amp," said: "All I had to do was catch it and cruise."

No freshman enjoyed a more spectacular season than Walker experienced in 1980. Georgia would win every close game, including a 17-10 victory over Notre Dame for the national championship in the Sugar Bowl. It was the first undefeated and untied team in Athens since 1946.

To win the close games, there had to be contributors other than "Humble Herschel," as he was known. He could power-off tackle, shedding tacklers and blasting into the secondary and beyond, but his teammates were also making big plays that contributed decisively to the undefeated season.

After Tennessee, Texas A&M fell 42-0 in Athens. Clemson was next, and the Tigers—still smarting after losing Walker to the recruiting wars—were primed to pull off an upset between the hedges.

Perhaps they would have succeeded had it not been for Scott Woerner. On that day, the Tigers focused on Walker and the offense, holding Georgia to a single rushing touchdown, a one-yard plunge by Buck Belue following Woerner's return of a Clemson interception to the Tigers' two-yard line.

Woerner had earlier returned a touchdown of 67 yards for Georgia's first score. On the subsequent interception, his legs cramped before he could reach the Clemson end zone following a 98-yard return.

Rex Robinson added two field goals, and Jeff Hipp, a native of Columbia, South Carolina, made a critical interception. Georgia was the victor, 20-16.

Texas Christian University was next, and the game became a yawner in the second half, with Georgia triumphing 34-3. Ole Miss tried hard a week later, but the Dogs won 28-21. Vanderbilt fell 41-0 in Georgia's fifth straight home game, and Kentucky was wiped out 27-0 in Lexington.

Believe it or not (Ripley probably wouldn't), up to that point in the year Georgia had yet to appear on television. Finally, however, the cameras arrived for the big home game against South Carolina.

(Below left) Buck Belue, center, helped lead Georgia to the 1980 National Championship with a 12-0 record. (Below right) Defensive back Scott Woerner (No. 19), a future College Football Hall of Famer, played a key role on the way to the national title.

BULLDOGS

The Heisman hype that year was focused on the Gamecocks' George Rogers, but it was Herschel Walker who would win the head-to-head duel—and from the Georgia point of view, Walker who should have received the trophy based on the statistical story. In addition to outgaining Rogers 219-168 yards, Walker scored 15 touchdowns on the season to Rogers' 14. Walker gained 1,616 yards on 274 attempts, while it took 324 attempts for Rogers to gain 1,894. Walker had 35 runs of more than 10 yards, and he ran for

more than 200 yards four times. Most of all, he led his team to the National Championship.

It was another case of Heisman injustice. It wasn't as bad as Trippi's experience in 1946, when the trophy went to Army's Glenn Davis, but Walker deserved to win the Heisman his first season. His freshman status, in fact, was probably the reason he didn't win—not enough voters could bring themselves to vote for a freshman. Walker would win the prized trophy in 1982.

Of course, when the cameras arrived for the South Carolina game, it was unknown who would win the 1980 Heisman. All eyes were on Rogers. In the fourth quarter, with Georgia leading 13-10, the Gamecocks mounted a drive, Rogers ripping off big yards until he reached the Bulldogs' 16-yard line. On the next play, Scott Woerner grabbed Rogers's elbow, loosening his grip. Dale Carver forced the ball out, and Tim Parks recovered to stop the visitors' last threat—two more unsung heroes making a contribution.

(Left) Bulldog running back Herschel Walker is considered to be one of the best college football players in history. In 1982, he was the second Georgia football player to win the Heisman Trophy. (Below) Herschel Walker's image appeared on the cover of Sports Illustrated during three consecutive years.

November 8, 1980: Georgia 26, Florida 21, at Jacksonville. Arguably the biggest play in Georgia history, and certainly in the Dooley era, was Buck Belue's 93-yard completion to Lindsay Scott. The touchdown enabled Georgia to get to and win the National Championship game. There was more work to be done, but that play snatched victory from the jaws of defeat.

With Walker carrying the ball, the Bulldogs moved downfield to the Carolina one-yard line, where Walker was stopped on fourth down. But the damage was done—the drive had effectively killed the clock. Jeff Hipp sealed the victory with an interception, three plays later.

The Bulldogs had left everything on the field, which is what it takes to win important games like that. The bad news was that the Bulldogs were unlikely to render a peak performance in a critical game the next week in Jacksonville. They would be up, they would play hard, but emotionally it is difficult to turn in a peak performance two weeks in a row.

Dooley's Dawgs showed what they were made of by coming from behind to defeat the Gators 26-21. With 1:35 left on the clock, Florida punted out of bounds at the Bulldogs' eight-yard line. The Gator fans began to celebrate. The Florida players got caught up in the celebration—a couple of defensive backs did the funky chicken when the punt went out of bounds. Not only is it unwise to celebrate victory with time on the clock, it was especially foolish to move into that mode with the Bulldogs of 1980.

On third down and 11, quarterback Buck Belue dropped back and looked for a receiver. As a hard-charging Gator was bearing down on him, Nat Hudson peeled off the line of scrimmage and knocked the defender out of the way. Belue found Lindsay Scott coming over the middle on a hash route (down and in, hitching on the hash mark). Belue's pass was high but on target. Lindsay jumped, caught the ball, turned, and headed to the sideline. The other end, Chuck Jones, shielded two defenders from the play, keeping

(Top) Walker was named All-America in 1982. (Above) Walker's No. 34 jersey and battle-scarred helmet today reside in UGA's athletic archives.

the Gators from catching Lindsay, who hit the sideline and sprinted to goal and to glory—93 yards. That play, tied with two others, remains the longest-pass play for a touchdown in Bulldog history. Add Chuck Jones and Nat Hudson to the list of unsung heroes without whom there would have been no National Championship.

(Above) Coach Dooley poses with Georgia Gov. George Busbee (left) before boarding a plane to New Orleans to take on Notre Dame's Fighting Irish.

Georgia had done the unlikely—left everything on the field, two games in a row. Would the Dawgs have enough left to pull it off three weekends in a row? And at Auburn?

They did, but it took a big play to spark the team to victory. In the second quarter, Greg Bell, a Birmingham native, broke through the defense and blocked a punt that was picked up by tackle Freddie Gilbert, who sprinted pell-mell on a 27-yard return for a touchdown. The Bulldogs gained momentum and

were the victors, 31–21. Georgia had gone into the game ranked number one in the country, a position that had come about when Georgia Tech, the weekend of the Florida game, pulled off an "upset tie" of Notre Dame, 3–3, in Atlanta.

Georgia was poised to become the collegiate football champion of 1980. All that was required was, first, to dispose of Georgia Tech (38–20), the team that had enabled the Bulldogs to gain the number-one ranking; and then, to go to the Sugar Bowl and beat the team Tech had knocked *out* of the number-one ranking—the Irish of Notre Dame.

This was a heady and unparalleled moment, and the slogan "How 'Bout Them Dawgs?" gained traction nationally. This overachieving bunch had for their centerpiece a precocious freshman named Herschel Walker. Some were saying it was Georgia's finest hour.

Then, on the way to the Sugar Bowl, a funny thing happened. Auburn sought to hire Dooley as head coach and athletic director. He was interested. After all, Auburn was his alma mater. Further, his relationship with the president of the University of Georgia, Fred Davison, had cooled.

Though Davison was a passionate fan and supporter of athletics, he held the opinion that one man should not be both athletic director and head football coach. When Joel Eaves retired in 1979, Davison considered offering the athletic directorship to the faculty chairman of athletics, a man with no experience in the sports arena. Dooley objected but offered a compromise plan that called for two athletic directors: an athletic director for sports and an athletic director for administration. It worked because Dooley understood the art of compromise. In truth, as AD for sports, he was the de facto athletic director, making all of the critical decisions. With a split developing among the Georgia people. This compromise enabled Davison to save face.

Initially, the Auburn opportunity seemed appealing, but as time went by, Dooley began to lean more toward staying put. He didn't ask for a lot of money, but a deal was struck that his house, owned by the GSEF, would become his. The other key issue was the athletic directorship. Dooley stayed, but not without irritating a lot of Georgia alumni who never really got over his flirting with Auburn—especially with the Bulldogs so close to winning a National Championship. He had rained on their parade, and a lot of good and loyal Dawgs were insulted—but, as always, winning solves most problems.

When the issue was settled, the Bulldogs once again focused on beating Notre Dame. To emerge victorious in New Orleans, Georgia would have to give a peak performance. They had a month to prepare. Auburn's courtship of Dooley was not the only funny thing to happen as they trained, though it was probably the least pleasant. The other oddity was that a little-known scholar-athlete from Huntsville, Texas, kept blocking field-goal attempts in practice. Terry Hoage had not been highly recruited, but he would become one of Georgia's most accomplished players by the time he left. He came of age on the practice field that December, and gained a roster spot for the final game of the season. Hoage deftly blocked a Notre Dame field goal in the first quarter, making one of the critical plays that enabled Georgia to win and become National Champion.

(Below) Between 1981 and 1984, Georgia kicker Kevin Butler amassed an impressive College Football Hall of Fame career before going on to play for the Chicago Bears.

Herschel Walker scored two touchdowns, but the big story—although nobody knew it at the time—was that he took 34 snaps with a dislocated shoulder, gaining 150 yards against a Notre Dame offense that had vowed it would not give up a hundred yards to the freshman tailback.

Following a Rex Robinson field goal, brothers Bob and Steve Kelly combined to come up with the ball on the ensuing kickoff when the Irish failed to cover the kick—the longest onside kick in history—contributing to the season-long script of everybody doing his part to contribute to victory. It always seemed that another no-name player would surface and make a key play. Walker got his yards and touchdowns—naturally, that was important. He was the big gun, but the "little guys" like the Kelly brothers were just as important, making consequential plays at critical junctures.

With time running out and Notre Dame behind 17-10 and threatening to score, it was Scott Woerner who intercepted an Irish pass at the Bulldogs' 34-yard line, where the Bulldogs ran out the clock. Walker won the Most Valuable Player trophy, but there should have been two trophies given that day—one for Walker and one for Scott Woerner.

In 1981, Georgia, led by Walker, Belue, Hoage, and Woerner, lost only one game: to a vengeful Clemson team when the Bulldogs turned the ball over a devastating nine times to lose to the eventual national champions, 13-3.

Georgia averaged 32 points a game on offense that year and gave up an average of 8.9 points per game on defense. It was their first year without Erk as the defensive chieftain. Following the National Championship, he'd chosen to direct Georgia Southern (where he would win three National Championships and emotionally captivate Statesboro as he had Athens). It was hard to replace a man like Erk, but the Bulldog players wiped the tears from their eyes and set about playing the same kind of unyielding, ball-hawking defense they'd been known for. The most points they gave up on the season, 21, were scored by Florida against the defense of Bill Lewis, who'd taken over as coordinator. The Bulldogs won again anyway, 26-21, the same score as the year before.

For the second year in a row the season ended with a trip to the Sugar Bowl, this time to face Pittsburgh. As the clock was running out the Dogs were leading Dan Marino and the Panthers 20-17. Then Marino completed a long pass for a touchdown to give Pittsburgh a 24-20 victory.

The loss of Erk to Georgia Southern was bad enough, but the Bulldogs were to lose another irreplaceable star. Nobody knew it at the outset, but 1982 would be Walker's last year. It would be another undefeated regular season. Walker broke a thumb in preseason practice, but Georgia was able to win a close one over Clemson on national television in

No. 14, Terrell "Terry" Hoage, seen here in the 1982 game against Brigham Young University, was a two-time consensus All-America player. Vince Dooley was quoted as saying that Hoage was "the best defensive player I've ever coached and maybe the best one I've ever seen." After graduation, he played for the New Orleans Saints.

---

10 BIG GAMES REMEMBERED: 1964–1988

January 2, 1984: Georgia 10, Texas 9, at Dallas. Trailing No. 2 Texas 9-3 late, Georgia got one more opportunity when the Bulldogs recovered a fumbled punt. Quarterback John Lastinger scored the only touchdown of the game, a run of 17 yards with a few seconds left on the clock. When he saw the official's upraised arms, signaling a touchdown, Lastinger said aloud, "Glory, Glory to Ole Georgia!"

(Top) Enclosing the east end zone stands of Sanford Stadium in 1981 created an additional 19,000 seats and brought the stadium's total capacity to 82,122. (Above) James Jackson (No. 14) carries the ball against Vanderbilt in 1986.

quarterback, was not a veteran passer. The Dawgs scored 23 points, but Todd Blackledge led the Nittany Lions to 27 points and victory.

During a night of bargaining, negotiating, and coercing, the USFL's New Jersey Generals successfully arm-twisted Herschel Walker into signing a document that would cause Georgia to declare him ineligible. Walker was off to a new life, and the entire campus was devastated and heartbroken.

It was tough losing the best running back in the country. What made it worse was that his departure left Georgia without a capable replacement. Although the talent level had dipped, however, the Bulldogs still knew how to win. Lastinger, a gutsy performer, led an offense that would score two or more touchdowns until the Florida game in Jacksonville. Nonetheless, the Dawgs prevailed 10-9.

Two years earlier, when Walker could dominate without question, Georgia had driven 95 yards in 17 plays to defeat Florida 26-21, the final score in 1980. Those 95 yards became known as "The Drive," and nobody thought it could ever be topped. Lastinger and the Bulldog offense pulled it off. He led Georgia 99 yards in 16 plays for a touchdown and a 10-9 victory—the first of two 10-9 victories that were the highlights of the first year after Walker's departure.

Against Auburn in Athens, Bo Jackson led Pat Dye's team to a 13-7 victory, killing Bulldog hopes for a fourth consecutive SEC title. A late interception by Tony Flack saved the Tech game in Atlanta, 27-24, and gained the Bulldogs an invitation to play second-ranked Texas in the Cotton Bowl.

The Longhorns were heavy favorites and have been kicking themselves ever since. Miami upset Nebraska that night in the Orange Bowl—if Texas had beaten Georgia that afternoon, the Longhorns could have been crowned national champions.

The Bulldog defense bent but never broke, holding Texas to three field goals that day. The Longhorn defense was even tougher, holding Georgia to a Kevin Butler field goal. Late in the fourth quarter, Texas fumbled a punt that was recovered by Gary Moss at the Texas 23-yard line.

On third down, offensive coordinator George Haffner called for Lastinger to run the option against a Texas defense that had been unyielding all afternoon.

the opener, 13-7. With only four days to prepare for Brigham Young in Athens, the Bulldogs were not in peak form against the visitors from Utah, but won the tight encounter 17-14. The Auburn game on November 13, 1982, was a nail biter. Auburn, trailing 19-14, saw a fourth-down pass broken up in the end zone in the closing minute of play, causing commentator Larry Munson to scream, "They broke it up. Oh, look at the sugar falling from the sky!"

Georgia was ranked number one when it lined up against Penn State in the Sugar Bowl. Walker, distracted by overtures from the USFL, didn't play up to par. John Lastinger, a wide receiver moved to

January 1, 1989: Georgia 34, Michigan State 27, at Jacksonville. While he had already won his milestone 200th game, Vince Dooley wanted to leave coaching a winner. The "Silver Seniors" made it happen. The Spartans were tough, but Dooley's Dawgs would not be denied. It was one of Dooley's sweetest victories in a career of big wins.

The Valdosta senior dashed 17 yards and scored just inside the pylon. Butler's extra point gave Georgia its second 10-9 victory of the season. Today you can ask a Bulldog fan the time, and he will always say, "In Texas, it is ten to nine."

From that point, Georgia would fall into a pattern of fewer wins—seven in 1984 and 1985, and eight in 1986. With bowl victories the next two years, the win total reached nine. Dooley considered that it was time to relinquish the coaching mantle and concentrate on upgrading Georgia's overall athletic program, emphasizing widespread facility expansion and development.

In December of 1988, he announced that he would no longer coach the Bulldog football team and that he was considering a run for the governor's office.

His last two games were memorable. His team defeated Georgia Tech in Athens, 24-3, for his 200th win. He would go out on top in the Gator Bowl with a 34-27 victory over Michigan State.

The Dooley era was Georgia's greatest. Garnering a National Championship and six SEC titles, Dooley ball was winning ball. When he laid down the coach's mantle, Hall of Famer Vince Dooley, at 201-77-10, was Georgia's winningest coach.

(Above) Coach Dooley during the twilight of his UGA coaching career. (Opposite page) When the UGA cheerleaders burst through the "Go You Silver Britches" banner in 1985 they had one of mascot Uga's favorite possessions in tow—a giant fire hydrant.

GO YOU
SILVER

NEXT: From Goff to Donnan to Richt. Finally winning the SEC again. Pollack the playmaker. Stafford comes of age.

"FINISH THE DRILL"

1989–2006
RECORD: 147 WINS, 74 LOSSES, 1 TIE

Mark Richt took a stumbling Georgia program and turned it into an annual SEC title contender.

At the time Vince Dooley retired from coaching, he was considering a run for the governor's office. He agreed with the university's president, Chuck Knapp, to serve as an advisor and to assist with the administrative transition within the Athletic Association until he could finalize campaign details.

Plainly speaking, things weren't good, and committing classic faux pas became the order of the day. A coach who was firmly established at another school couldn't be easily wooed to UGA when he didn't know who his athletic director was going to be. Knapp, inexperienced with such an assignment, tried to be ecumenical and involved too many people. He failed to follow the rule of thumb: hire the AD first and let *him* lead the search for a coach. Whoever heard of an unqualified board hiring the coach and, as if there were nothing to it, just happening on a qualified athletic director? Dick Sheridan, then at North Carolina State, later told me, "When I interviewed for the job, I was interviewed by the entire athletic board. I thought to myself, 'What a hell of a job, but what a ridiculous process.'"

Erk Russell, the people's choice, really didn't want the job, though he wanted the right of first refusal. And his reluctance was mainly due, as it was with everyone else, to the fact that he didn't know who his athletic director would be. "One of the reasons I'm not interested," Erk said in my first conversation with him, "is that I would have to fire every coach up there. I would bring my own staff."

Dooley was influential behind the scenes but did not take the lead or manage the search as would have been the case if he were the athletic director or interim AD. It was a classic case of how *not* to hire a coach. As time went by, the decision was made to hire from within. At one point, linebacker coach Dale Strahm had the job, but he was the subject of intense jealousy within the staff. His candidacy, with some last-minute political maneuvering behind the scenes, went up in smoke—certainly through no fault of his. He was well qualified.

Assistant head coach George Haffner, not only a fine coach but also a very honest and genuine person, was unpopular with the alumni, who found fault with his play calling and who (as they always do) began

(Preceding page) Mark Richt took over as head coach at Georgia in 2001. Richt played quarterback at the University of Miami, and later served as Bobby Bowden's offensive coordinator at Florida State. (Above) Richt established right away that he had a special touch when it came to coaching, recruiting and managing a football team.

BULLDOGS

1989–2006

BULLDOGS

clamoring for a Georgia man. In the end, Ray Goff, popular with a large section of the alumni and holding high marks from many of them as a recruiter, got the job. His tenure became a matter of on-the-job training. Goff had never been a coordinator; he had not disciplined himself for the serious and detailed study of football. Goff did understand the importance of reaching out to the Bulldog nation, but unfortunately, in the end, that was not enough to carry the day.

Following a 6-6 start that included a victory over Florida and a Peach Bowl invitation, Georgia posted a 4-7 record. Goff hired offensive coordinator Wayne McDuffie. The Bulldogs then became attractive to Eric Zeier, the top quarterback in the state, with McDuffie installing the Florida State offense.

In 1991, Zeier led the Dogs to a 9-3 season and a 24-15 victory over Arkansas in the Independence Bowl. It got better a year later, when the Bulldogs won 10 games and defeated Ohio State in the Citrus Bowl, 21-14. It appeared that the Bulldogs were headed in the right direction.

(Top left) Former UGA quarterback Ray Goff had been working at UGA as an assistant coach for seven years when he was tapped to replace retiring head coach Vince Dooley in 1989. Goff was fired in 1995 with a 46-34-1 record. (Top right) Jim Donnan became the Bulldogs' head coach in 1996. During his four-year reign, Donnan led Georgia to four consecutive bowl victories, but was fired in November 2000.
(Left) Working as a broadcaster since the 1940s, iconic and colorful Larry Munson started calling Bulldog games in 1966 and continued until his retirement in 2008. Munson passed away Nov. 20, 2011.

10 BIG GAMES REMEMBERED: 1989–2006

January 1, 1993: Georgia 21, Ohio State 14, at Orlando. Running back Garrison Hearst rushed for 163 yards as the Bulldogs won 10 games for the first time in 10 years. The Citrus Bowl victory brought Georgia a final ranking of No. 8.

When Sanford Stadium's west end zone stands were partially enclosed in 1991 more than 4,000 new seats were added, bringing the old stadium's total capacity to 85,434.

However, the bottom fell out in 1993, Zeier's senior year. It was a 5-6 campaign that was followed by 6-4-1 and 6-6 seasons. The good news was that Goff's teams had defeated Georgia Tech five years in a row. Even so, Dooley, who stayed as AD, felt that he had to make a change, releasing his former quarterback and assistant coach in late 1995.

He then hired Glen Mason of Kansas. Mason was head coach for eight days, then had a change of heart while flying with his Jayhawk team to Honolulu for the Oahu Bowl.

Impressed with Jim Donnan's knowledge of football during the interview process, Dooley offered him the job. The Marshall head coach had, in essence, come through the process a runner-up.

Donnan's teams won 40 and lost 19, for a 67% winning percentage—not bad, but not good, either, when his teams did not seriously contend for the SEC East title. His 1997 team beat Florida 37-17, and in 1996 at Auburn, in the first overtime game in the history of the SEC, the Bulldogs defeated Auburn 56-49. Those were Donnan's high-water marks.

There is no question that the competitive balance across college football teams today is greater than ever. There are more good players with talent and speed, and owing to existing scholarship limitations, no team can stockpile enough players to dominate on a long-term basis. Anybody with objectivity, sound reasoning, and plain good sense (which is often missing when things are not so good on the field and the emotions take over) clearly knows that winning does not come easy.

Nonetheless, UGA president Michael Adams orchestrated a change, and Donnan was fired within a fortnight of his third straight loss to Georgia Tech on November 25, 2000. He went out a winner, however, coaching his team to a 37-14 victory over Virginia at the Jeep Oahu Bowl on Christmas Eve.

Dooley then hired Mark Richt, who right away established that he had a special touch when it came to coaching, recruiting, and managing a football team. He had prepared himself to be a head coach of a major program, and it showed.

There was nothing to dislike about the handsome and laid-back Richt. He arrived with a young and attractive family. Two of his children were newly adopted from Ukraine, and the family presented an image of altruism and selflessness. He spoke modestly and humbly. He underscored spiritual values and togetherness. He was all about family, and once his team bought into his philosophy and system, positive results began to take place on the field.

In Richt's first season, his team won eight games. Except for close losses to South Carolina and Auburn, Georgia could have gotten into the SEC Championship game. There was plenty to celebrate, however, as his team defeated Tennessee in Knoxville and Georgia Tech in Atlanta.

(Above) In this centennial year cartoon by UGA alum Jack Davis, the Bulldog of 1892 shakes hands with the Bulldog of 1992.

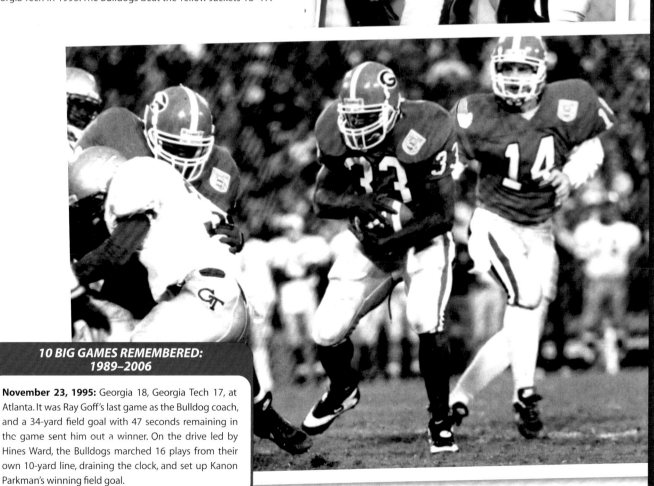

(Above) Kicker John Kasay graduated in 1990 before being drafted in 1991 by the Seattle Seahawks. (Right) Wide receiver Andre Hastings (No. 1) and running back Garrison Hearst (No. 5) in 1991. (Below) Terrell Davis (No. 33) carrying the ball against Georgia Tech in 1995. The Bulldogs beat the Yellow Jackets 18–17.

10 BIG GAMES REMEMBERED: 1989–2006

November 23, 1995: Georgia 18, Georgia Tech 17, at Atlanta. It was Ray Goff's last game as the Bulldog coach, and a 34-yard field goal with 47 seconds remaining in the game sent him out a winner. On the drive led by Hines Ward, the Bulldogs marched 16 plays from their own 10-yard line, draining the clock, and set up Kanon Parkman's winning field goal.

The next year, after a long and disappointing wait of 20 years, his second team won the SEC title over Arkansas, 30-3, in the championship game. Then it was on to the Sugar Bowl, where his former team, Florida State, became the Bulldogs' 13th victim in a serendipitous season. Hail to the Richt Dawgs!

There are many highlights of Richt's Georgia start, but after Dooley retired as athletic director in 2004, he left behind a specter of doubt. Richt had taken the Bulldogs to the SEC Championship, but would he be able to maintain winning consistency in the big games?

From the start, Richt emphasized team spirit. "All for one and one for all" is a slogan that may be trite and as old as the hills, but a football team that embraces and functions with this basic philosophy in mind is a team that has the best championship opportunity. Richt made no reference to Georgia's past except to laud the championship tradition. He had always told his friends privately that Georgia had to be one of the best opportunities in football for an aspiring coach.

The Florida State football team has spent its pre-game Friday nights in Thomasville, Georgia, for years. Known for its unrivaled quail-hunting plantations, Thomasville is also big on golf. In addition to being an outdoorsman's mecca, Thomasville boasts a high school football team—also known as the Bulldogs—that has produced many outstanding college players.

Richt had recruited players from such schools in Georgia for FSU, and was familiar with the level of football competition and coaching in the state. He concluded that high school football in the Peach State was as good as it is anywhere. Florida might have more blue-chip players with a greater population, but, if a coach could recruit the best 25 players in Georgia on an annual basis, he

All-America quarterback Eric Zeier finished his UGA career with an astonishing 67 school records and 18 SEC records. In 1995 he was drafted by the Cleveland Browns.

(Left) Defensive back Kirby Smart intercepted two passes during 1997's 37-17 victory over Florida. A first team All-SEC selection as a senior, he had 13 career interceptions at Georgia. Smart got his start in coaching at UGA in 1999 as an administrative assistant, and would circle back to Georgia before the 2016 season. (Below) Richt's first Bulldog team in 2001 won eight games, including victories over Tennessee and Georgia Tech.

10 BIG GAMES REMEMBERED: 1989–2006

October 6, 2001: Georgia 26, Tennessee 24, at Knoxville. The CBS cameras were on hand, and the last two minutes were electrifying. With the Bulldogs clinging to a three-point lead, Tennessee scored on a 62-yard screen pass to retake the lead 24-20 with 44 seconds left. Redshirt freshman David Greene drove the Bulldogs 69 yards for the winning score, a six-yard pass to Verron Haynes with five seconds left to play.

would line up talent as capable as that on any team. Richt was overwhelmingly confident of that, which is why he placed a premium on quality recruiting.

He had admired the teams of Vince Dooley, although Dooley used the run to set up the pass—the opposite of Richt, who used the pass to set up the run. And it didn't take Richt long to identify with the Georgia people as well as with the school's tradition. He was popular from the start, with his laid-back, unassuming personality from which emanated feelings of goodwill and good tidings to all. He had an easy way about him. People felt comfortable in his presence. The welcome mat was always out.

There was no mistake—Richt wanted Bulldog alumni and friends to be aware that he was happy to be at a place where he felt that winning could be achieved on the highest level. He wanted them to know that he appreciated Georgia's tradition and that he was proud to be a part of it.

When he set about upgrading the appearance of the team quarters in the Butts-Mehre Building, he placed emphasis on the Georgia "G," a symbol he wanted to be visually dominant. Bowl trophies and championship plaques that confirmed Georgia's success were given a place of prominence.

Defensive end David Pollack was the second Bulldog in UGA history to become a three-time All-American. In 2005, he was drafted by the Cincinnati Bengals but suffered a career-ending injury early in his second season. Pollack has enjoyed a successful broadcasting career since 2008.

Richt's first objective was to instill team-first principles. His motto, "Finish the Drill," became a catchphrase that turned into the theme of his first championship team, in 2002.

In his first five years, Richt's teams were exciting on offense and big playmakers on defense, with an emphasis on the kicking game. His teams won two SEC titles (2002 and 2005) and played for the championship in 2003, losing to LSU. After five seasons his 80% winning percentage was the best among league coaches.

A late pass gave South Carolina victory in Athens in the second game of Richt's first season. Florida won 24-10 in Jacksonville, but the game that ripped at Richt was the Auburn game, when his Bulldogs failed to get the ball into the end zone in the closing seconds and lost 24-17. It was a classic case of missed opportunity—a new experience for Richt.

There was considerable criticism of clock management in the frustrating loss. Richt had called for a run at the Auburn goal line, but a lineman missed a block, and Auburn stopped Jasper Sanks short of the end zone. If the block had been successful, Sanks would have scored easily, but because the play failed, the second-guessers asked why not throw in that situation to "protect" the clock.

During the off-season, Richt called in a well-traveled offensive coach, Homer Smith, for a short course on clock management. This was a signal not only that the young Bulldog coach was unafraid to admit that he'd made a mistake, but that he wasn't too proud to do something about it and say so publicly.

Pollack's childhood friend and UGA roommate, quarterback David Green (No. 14), completed his Georgia career as the winningest quarterback in NCAA Division 1 history. Green's record surpassed the one previously held by Tennessee's Peyton Manning. In 2005, he was drafted by the Seattle Seahawks.

BULLDOGS

1989–2006

10 BIG GAMES REMEMBERED: 1989–2006

September 14, 2002: Georgia 13, South Carolina 7, at Columbia. A memorable game, but more memorable was Davey Pollack's steal of an attempted pass for a touchdown to ignite a Bulldog victory in which the defense won the day. The Dawgs failed to score an offensive touchdown, but Billy Bennett kicked two field goals, and with the game on the line, the defense forced a fumble at the Bulldogs' two-yard line to claim victory.

As the team absorbed his preachments, it became a team bent on overachieving. The Richt Dawgs defeated Georgia Tech in Atlanta to halt a three-game winning streak, and spirits were high. But buoyant spirits sagged considerably when the best bowl invitation this eight-win team could get was the Music City Bowl. The team had aspired to a more attractive bowl. Based on their record, they deserved what they preferred; when it didn't come, there was not a lot of enthusiasm for playing Boston College on a cold and windy night in Nashville.

Over the winter, as Richt and his staff began to plan for his second year, Georgia fans celebrated in the confidence that they had a coach who could win big games and who could get the Dawgs into the SEC Championship Game. There was

(Top left) Quarterback Lavonya Quintelle "Quincy" Carter played baseball for two seasons with the Chicago Cubs before coming to UGA in 1998. He was drafted by the Dallas Cowboys in 2001. (Top right) Lightning-fast linebacker Rodney "Boss" Bailey was drafted by the Detroit Lions in 2003. (Left) Defensive lineman Richard Seymour (No. 93) converses with teammate and defensive tackle Marcus Stroud (No. 97). Seymour and Stroud both went on to long NFL careers after being drafted in 2001's first round, by New England and Jacksonville, respectively. Seymour was named to seven Pro Bowls, Stroud three.

10 BIG GAMES REMEMBERED: 1989–2006

November 16, 2002: Georgia 24, Auburn 21, at Auburn. It was fourth down and 13 yards to go at the Auburn 13-yard line when David Greene hit Michael Johnson for the winning touchdown with 1:25 remaining. The win gave Georgia the SEC East title and a trip to the SEC Championship Game it the Georgia Dome at Atlanta.

2002 SEC CHAMPIONS

10 BIG GAMES REMEMBERED:
1989–2006

December 7, 2002: Georgia 30, Arkansas 3, at Atlanta. A blocked punt by Decory Bryant propelled Georgia to a 17-0 first-quarter lead in the SEC Championship Game as Musa Smith scored two touchdowns, Ben Watson had three scores, and Billy Bennett kicked three field goals. The Dawg defense held Arkansas to a single field goal in the third quarter.

the widespread sense that a different atmosphere prevailed in Athens—this coaching staff was hungry for a championship.

Much of the enthusiasm was due not only to the defeat of Georgia Tech in 2001 but also to the come-from-behind victory over Tennessee in Knoxville, where Georgia hadn't won since Dooley was coaching. Richt, by this time, had sold his team on the fact that they were good enough to beat anybody and that they could win anywhere in the SEC.

Late in the quarter, Georgia had the lead 20-17 when the Volunteers scored on a screen pass to regain the lead, 24-20. Gloom did not envelop the Georgia sideline. Richt gathered the offense around him and gave them the plan for their last possession from the Georgia 42-yard line with only 42 seconds left on the clock. The following sequence of plays tells the most uplifting story of Richt's initial season, in which pride in Georgia football was restored:

Greene pass to Gary for 13 yards, first down.
Greene pass to Johnson, incomplete.
Greene pass to McMichaels for 26 yards, first down.
Greene pass to McMichaels for 14 yards, first down.
Greene pass to Verron Haynes for six yards and the
  winning touchdown.

For those among the 107,592 fans who were wearing orange, it was a trip from ecstasy to agony. And there had been some Georgia fans—o ye of little faith!—who, following Tennessee's late score, had dashed to their cars in order to beat the traffic out of town. It was a lesson not to forget: don't leave the game when Georgia has a chance with Mark Richt coaching the Bulldogs.

Georgia had beaten Tennessee in Knoxville in Richt's first year. And they had pulled off a pulsating victory with a redshirt freshman quarterback, David Greene. Greene would go on to become the winningest NCAA Division 1 quarterback of all time, with 42 victories on his collegiate watch.

2002 SEC Championship ring.

In Richt's second season there would be six close games, and his Bulldogs would win five of them, losing only to Florida, 20-13, in Jacksonville. Richt's teams in the first five years of the millennium would beat every rival on the schedule, with the toughest game coming in Jacksonville against the Gators.

The opening game between the hedges in 2002 would be one to remember, with Clemson going down 31-28. Richt came up with a gutsy call late in that game that brought victory. Georgia had the lead, but Richt chose to gamble on the fourth down instead of punting—he didn't want to give the ball back to Clemson. Musa Smith dove over the top for a first down, and the Bulldogs ran out the clock.

No team on the schedule would score 28 points on the Bulldog defense thereafter. The offense would average 32.8 points per game, as the Bulldogs claimed their first SEC title in 20 years. It would be the first visit ever to the Georgia Dome in Atlanta for the SEC title game, in which the Dawgs whacked Arkansas 30-3. Richt, recognizing that Georgia played in the toughest conference in college football, nonetheless wanted to make trips to the playoff game a habit.

In the Nokia Sugar Bowl, Georgia defeated Florida State 26-13 and finished the season with a No. 3 national ranking. The Bulldogs had achieved their objective. They had *finished the drill*.

These Dawgs had character, and they represented a new era in Athens. They would win 10 or more games a year for the next three seasons. They had all of Athens believing in them, believing they would contend for the SEC East every year. The entire state would get caught up in the success of Richt and his football team.

Richt—focusing on church, family, and the Bulldogs, in that order—made the Bulldog nation aware that he could not only produce winning teams but also recruit the players that would make the Bulldogs title contenders on an annual basis.

Leading the team to new heights were a number of overachievers, but the spotlight focused more often than not on quarterback Greene and defensive All-America end David Pollack. Greene was on hand when Richt arrived, but he recruited Pollack.

Inseparable friends since grade school, they would become known as the "Beloved Dawgs." Both were named David, so Pollack took the name Davey to distinguish between the two. To play for the championship two out of four years and miss out on a third by one lousy game was unbearable, and big plays became expected—by players and coaches—with Richt's first recruiting class.

(Left) After graduating from UGA in 2003, offensive tackle Jon Stinchcomb was drafted by the New Orleans Saints.

Sanford Stadium was again expanded in 2003. An additional upper deck with 5,500 new seats was added to Sanford's north side, and the following year, 27 SkySuites were also added.

Greene, the classy lefthander, could find a way to get it done on offense, and Pollack was the most extraordinary big-play playmaker Georgia has had on defense in years—a lineman making plays in the tradition of defensive backs like Charley Trippi, Jake Scott, Scott Woerner, and Terry Hoage. For an end, unheard of!

He set the school record for career sacks with 36, and a listing of his plays—from sacks to blocked kicks to interceptions to tackles for loss—would number into the dozen of dozens.

So often, it was more than a big play, it was a *spectacular* play—the classic example coming at South Carolina in 2002, when he literally took the ball out of the Gamecock quarterback's hand as he started forward with his throwing motion. Pollack was credited with an interception, but it was the biggest heist since Jesse James. Game tapes showed the quarterback was dumbfounded, looking about for the ball—even he didn't know exactly what had happened. The ball was cradled to Pollack's stomach in the end zone.

Northwestern State had been conquered easily, 45-7, and so had New Mexico State, 41-10, when a big question surfaced as the Bulldogs prepared for Alabama at Tuscaloosa. Were the Dawgs man enough to beat Alabama? The author of that question was former Auburn coach Pat Dye, who had played for the Bulldogs under Wally Butts.

As soon as Dye's comments became public, it was a foregone conclusion that the issue would receive top billing on the Georgia locker-room bulletin board. The question was fervently discussed on radio talk shows throughout the week. The answer came on a hot afternoon at Bryant-Denny Stadium, when Georgia, trailing 25-24, took possession of the ball at Alabama's 34-yard line with 3:45 left on the clock.

In 2004, wide receiver Fred Gibson played a major role in helping to beat LSU 45–16. After a brief stint with the Miami Dolphins, Gibson was signed by the Atlanta Falcons in 2007.

In the Swahili language "Musa" means king, and in 2003, running back Musa Smith definitely lived up to the name. He was one of the Bulldogs' star players during the 26-13 Sugar Bowl victory against Florida State, rushing for 145 yards on 23 carries. Later that year, he was drafted by the Baltimore Ravens.

David Greene was cool under fire and his offensive line was bulldozing efficiently as he moved the team to the Alabama 15-yard line—milking the clock in the process—and Billy Bennett, the sure-footed kicker, booted a 32-yard field goal to bring about victory.

A week later in Athens, Tennessee wanted revenge and fought hard to get it, but the Bulldogs would not be denied. A blocked punt and a blocked field-goal attempt were the big plays in the Bulldogs' 18-13 victory, which was followed by walks in the park over Vandy, 48-17, between the hedges, and Kentucky at Lexington, 52-24.

With a scenario that would be played out again and again in Richt's first five years in Jacksonville, the favored Bulldogs lost a close one to Florida, 20-13. Mistakes on both sides of the ball were costly, but there were two SEC games left. The Bulldogs controlled their destiny. Things went smoothly when Ole Miss came to town and were dispatched 31-17, but a comeback was required at Auburn for the Dawgs to claim Mark Richt's first SEC Championship.

Greene's pass of 19 yards to Michael Johnson was as critical under-fire as a Bulldog team had experienced since 1959, when Fran Tarkenton threw to Bill Herron for a touchdown of 13 yards against Auburn in Athens. Both touchdowns were eerily similar. Fourth down, game on the line. A touchdown pass to an end lined up on the left side wins the game and brings about a championship. The only difference was that in 2002, the game was played in Auburn.

Before the 70-mile trip to the Georgia Dome and the SEC Championship, there was the matter of the state championship game to be played between the hedges. With CBS television cameras on hand, the Bulldogs have never been more dominant in the ancient series. Richt cleared the bench in the fourth

The 2003 win over Florida State marked Coach Richt's first bowl victory as UGA's head coach.

quarter as the Bulldogs were victorious 51-7 in a runaway.

In the SEC Championship Game, Georgia, again coming up with big plays, blocked the first punt of the game and scored a play later with 11:58 remaining in the first quarter to take a 7-0 lead over Arkansas. The Razorbacks never really threatened on offense, coming up with a field goal in the third quarter. The final score: 30-3.

The Bulldogs were SEC champions and would play Florida State in the Sugar Bowl. It was a game Richt wanted passionately to win, but he knew it would be another one of those "man-enough" challenges. In addition, there was the emotionally draining circumstance of competing against his longtime friends on the Seminole coaching staff. Beating your friends might be your objective, but it is not really a fun experience.

It was a close game, but a 71-yard interception return for a touchdown by Bruce Thornton in the second quarter put the Bulldogs up 10-7. FSU would not regain the lead, and Georgia had another championship ring to pass out—the Sugar Bowl championship, 26-13.

In 2003, Georgia reached the championship game again by winning 11 games, including a 41-14 pasting of Tennessee in Knoxville and an overtime defeat of Purdue, 34-27, in the Capital One Bowl at Orlando. The Bulldogs had to settle for the SEC East Championship, losing to LSU 34-13 in the title game at the Georgia Dome. It was the second loss of the season to a much-improved LSU, something that grated heavily on the Bulldog staff. At Baton Rouge, turnovers, mistakes, and failures in Georgia's kicking game had allowed the Tigers to survive 17-10.

That was all well and good for the Tigers, but they would be ambushed and thrashed soundly the next year in Athens. Payback would be sweet in 2004, but until then the Bulldogs would have to live with bitter disappointment over the winter. They knew they were better than they had performed—in both Baton Rouge and Atlanta.

With Greene and Pollack entering their senior seasons, ambitions were high—and so were the preseason ratings, which nonetheless did not reflect a true picture of the team. There were some shortages

(Left) Kicker Billy Bennett (No. 30) became the SEC's career scoring leader during the 2003 season. His 81 field goals set a league record. (Bottom) Despite being plagued with injuries, in 2004 wide receiver Reggie Brown (No. 1) led the Bulldogs in receptions. He caught an impressive 53 passes for 860 yards and six touchdowns. In 2005 he joined up with the Philadelphia Eagles.

10 BIG GAMES REMEMBERED: 1989–2006

October 30, 2004: Georgia 31, Florida 24, at Jacksonville. Frustration abated after seven years of losing to the Gators. Florida fought back in the final quarter, but Fred Gibson's fingertip catch in the end zone sealed the victory, with quarterback David Greene setting the school record for career touchdown responsibility with 72.

at certain positions, especially on defense, which had coordinator Brian VanGorder worried and doubtful of the preseason No. 3 national ranking.

The Dawg defense struggled at times against the option attack during the opener with Georgia Southern, and then Georgia fell behind South Carolina, 16-0. However, they had the resolve and leadership to fight back and leave Columbia with a 21-16 victory. Georgia next defeated Marshall 13-3 in a game in which the Bulldogs were not very impressive. There was good reason: LSU would be coming to town a week later. It was hard to focus on the team wearing green when gold and purple would pack the visitors' locker room at Sanford Stadium on October 2, 2004.

Coach Richt celebrates with his team after winning the 2005 SEC Championship Game against LSU in Atlanta.

Looking back on the Richt era, although his teams often have been primed for victory, it is without question that none have been more prepared mentally or peaked more perfectly than the team on the day they played the Tigers in 2004. Every upperclassman on the team was still smarting from the defeats of the season before. Practices were crisp and sharp, focus was keen and determined—the Dawgs were ready.

This was a fine LSU team, one that was ambitious under Nick Saban, a defensive-oriented and supremely ambitious coach with a confident and driven ego. The Tigers had championship dreams of their own, but they were soundly thrashed 45-16. "The Dawgs took us to the woodshed," said LSU assistant Kirby Smart, who had played at Georgia and would return to Athens as an assistant a year later.

The Bulldogs scored early and often, putting up points in every quarter. Greene was never more on target to sure-handed receivers like Reggie Brown and Fred Gibson, keeping the ball on offense 75 plays to LSU's 59. The final score, 45-16, was reflective of Georgia's complete dominance.

Before the sun had set the day the Bulldogs defeated LSU, Mark Richt began talking of the challenge that lay ahead. Tennessee was coming to town 0-3 versus Richt-coached teams, and the Bulldog coach knew that getting his players' collective feet back on the ground after slamming LSU would be no mean feat.

He realized that playing two peak games back to back was not an unremarkable challenge. Playing at home helped, but all week he had difficulty getting his team focused, unlike the week before. Just too many congratulatory salutes and laudatory slaps on the back. To win a championship, no team can live in the past—even for a week.

In 2001, quarterback Donald Eugene "D.J." Shockley was one of Coach Richt's first recruits. As a senior, he co-captained the Bulldogs during the 2005 SEC Championship year and was named MVP of the championship game.

The team would be ready to play, but rendering a peak performance was another matter. The Bulldogs fought hard, but they just missed winning, lacking that competitive sharpness needed in a big SEC game. A missed field goal, a kick return nullified by penalty, a touchdown pass disallowed when the receiver's foot was a couple of inches over the back of the end-zone line, were among a half dozen plays that, reversed, would have brought victory.

In the end, it is noteworthy that the Bulldogs were knocking on the door when time expired. A David Greene pass, which would have won the game, was intercepted when a receiver ran the wrong route. Tennessee prevailed 19-14, and the Dawgs would get no help from any other team in the league. They had to settle for the runner-up spot in the SEC East, even after beating Florida, Kentucky, and Auburn down the stretch.

The season ended on a high note. With 10 wins, the Dawgs finished ranked No. 6. They fought off a gallant effort by Georgia Tech in Athens in the rain, 19-13, and when Wisconsin closed the score to 24-21 with a late touchdown in the Outback Bowl, Greene and the Bulldogs killed the clock by not letting the Badgers have it back on the ensuing kickoff.

Pollack duplicated his feat at Columbia by sacking the Wisconsin quarterback and taking the ball away, finishing his sensational career in a blaze of glory in the Florida sunshine at Tampa.

When Georgia began spring drills in 2005, Greene and Pollack were gone. And so were Thomas Davis, Reggie Brown, Fred Gibson, and Odell Thurman. Quarterback D.J. Shockley had experience, but the team was his for the first time after backing up Greene for three seasons. There were doubters aplenty. Nobody expected the Bulldogs to win the SEC title, but that was exactly what happened.

(Below) The 2005 SEC Championship trophy can be seen today displayed in UGA's Butts-Mehre Heritage Hall.

**10 BIG GAMES REMEMBERED:
1989-2006**

December 3, 2005: Georgia 34, LSU 14, at Atlanta. Underdog Georgia, led by quarterback D.J. Shockley, trounced LSU 34-14 to win the SEC Championship Game. Shockley threw two touchdown passes to Sean Bailey and ran for another. Tim Jennings returned an interception for a touchdown and Brandon Coutu kicked a pair of field goals, as the Bulldogs dominated.

WESTERN
UNIVERSITY OF ALABAMA
UNIVERSITY OF ARKANSAS
AUBURN UNIVERSITY
LOUISIANA STATE UNIVERSITY
UNIVERSITY OF MISSISSIPPI
MISSISSIPPI STATE UNIVERSITY

EASTERN
UNIVERSITY OF FLORIDA
UNIVERSITY OF GEORGIA
UNIVERSITY OF KENTUCKY
UNIVERSITY OF SOUTH CAROLINA
UNIVERSITY OF TENNESSEE
VANDERBILT UNIVERSITY

UNIVERSITY OF GEORGIA
2005 CHAMPION

The Bulldogs won 10 games, highlighted by a 34-14 ambushing of LSU in the championship game. During the regular season, the Dawgs won again in Knoxville, defeating Tennessee 27-14. However, they lost to Florida, with Shockley sidelined by a knee injury suffered in a 23-20 victory over Arkansas. Auburn, with a late touchdown in which the Bulldog secondary missed an assignment, won in Athens, but the Dawgs were still the SEC East champions.

On the way to the SEC title in the Georgia Dome, the Bulldogs disposed of Georgia Tech for the fifth year in a row, 14-7, when Tim Jennings intercepted a Reggie Ball pass at the Georgia goal line in the final minutes of the game.

The third loss of the season came in a shootout in the Sugar Bowl, with West Virginia winning 38-35, succeeding with a surprise late fake punt. The Mountaineers knew that if Georgia and Shockley got the ball back, they would not be able to stop the Bulldogs, who had fallen behind 28-0 in the first half but gallantly fought back.

West Virginia became the overachievers, the underdogs who chafed at the suggestion that their Big East team didn't deserve their lofty Bowl Championship Series opportunity. Georgia entered the game without the mental peak it needed to play an upstart team like West Virginia.

Nonetheless, it was a stirring season with plenty to boast about over the winter, mainly because Shockley shut up all the critics and ended his career by leading his team to the SEC title.

In 2006, without a field-goal kicker in midseason and with a freshman quarterback, the Bulldogs slumped. They lost to Vanderbilt and Kentucky but rallied to defeat Auburn 37-15 and Georgia Tech 15-12.

(Above) Coach Richt carrying his son David, obviously a Pollack fan.

The sixth Richt season was one of slump and serendipity. With an unsettled quarterback situation, the Bulldogs won early but then became schizophrenic. In midseason you never knew which face, which cloak, the Dawgs would wear. Even with a 5-0 start, the Bulldogs struggled. Turnovers on offense seemed to constantly force the defense into back-to-the-wall challenges that resulted in breakdowns. The wheels simply fell off during the second half of the game in a devastating loss to Tennessee at home.

Then the worst followed, a homecoming loss to Vanderbilt—on a last-second field goal by the Commodores—followed by a similar fate against Kentucky in Lexington. The Wildcats scored late to cause a goalpost-tearing-down rush from the home-team fans. All the while, the Bulldog coaching staff labored under the depression of knowing that with a healthy placekicker the Bulldogs would have posted at least two more victories.

It was a new experience for Richt, but as we have been often reminded, all's well that ends well. Suddenly, freshman quarterback Matthew Stafford came of age.

He learned to make the percentage pass, protect the ball, and eliminate interceptions. At Auburn, the number-five-ranked Tigers were ambushed 37-15. With an open date, the Bulldogs healed a few wounds and were economical on both offense and defense in the finale between the hedges. For the sixth year in a row, Georgia Tech became a victim, 15-12. This made the Bulldogs attractive to the Chick-fil-A Bowl, but the challenge was formidable. The Dawgs were ready, however. They defeated ACC power Virginia Tech 31-24, coming back from a 21-3 halftime deficit.

Georgia's 3-0 finish was one of the best in Bulldog history. With favorable recruiting success on signing day, there was joy all around. "Matthew Stafford has experience and we've still got Mark Richt," drawled Robert Westmoreland, a Georgia fan from Ellijay.

What Richt accomplished so quickly was exceptional. He not only won big games and championships—he made football fun again at UGA. He spread goodwill and underscored that the power of positive thinking was able to trump all else. The future, however, is often very unpredictable.

(Below) Richt encourages his Bulldogs before a home game. (Opposite page) Richt gets doused after the 2007 Chick-fil-A Bowl victory in Atlanta.

December 30, 2006: Georgia 31, Virginia Tech 24, at Atlanta. After a field goal in the third quarter, Georgia's offense was jump-started by an onside kick as the Bulldogs scored 28 unanswered points in the second half in the Chick-fil-A Bowl. Freshman quarterback Matthew Stafford was the offensive MVP, and Tony Taylor, with two interceptions, was the defensive MVP in one of Georgia's greatest comebacks.

NEXT: Running on empty with 11 wins. Mark Richt: A damn good Dawg. A Smart hire. Turning it around quickly. 2017's surprise rise. Playing Bama for the title.

A Smart Transition

2007-2017
Record: 106 wins, 41 losses

"Our student-athletes will represent the university with class and integrity. We will demand that. Our teams will display great mental and physical toughness. We'll play with great confidence and pride on the field. We'll work toward this with relentless energy and passion, and I will demand that everyone in the organization does that."

— Georgia head coach Kirby Smart, prior to the 2016 season

decade or so ago, Georgia football experienced the ecstasy of victory and agony of defeat, which caused emotions to spike and deflate as inconsistency was often an interloper with hopes too often dashed.

The 2006 season, for example, resulted in the Bulldogs winning nine games, but could only be described as mediocre. Four Southeastern Conference losses brought on rampant frustration. Dating back to his second season as Georgia's head coach, Mark Richt had developed a pattern of winning 10 games and competing for the SEC East title. He seemed to always win the "state championship," and there was uplifting bowl success more often than not.

The SEC East was beginning to slip, however, in terms of competitiveness. That wouldn't be confirmed until Alabama, under Nick Saban, became established and subsequently dominant, setting a new standard in the SEC West.

By this time, however, you would have initiated a lot of heated arguments if you had suggested that Richt had won his last SEC title. Sadly, that was the case. He would get to the Georgia Dome twice more (2011 and 2012), but there would be no championship celebration until Kirby Smart's second season in 2017.

The most disappointing season was 2012 when the Bulldogs lost a heartbreaker to Alabama when they moved just outside the Tide goal line in the last minute of the final quarter of the SEC Championship Game; a deflected Aaron Murray pass was caught by Chris Conley at the 5-yard line as the clock ran out before Georgia was able to try one last scoring attempt. That was during the days of the old BCS system, which had played out that year to where the winner of the SEC title would play No. 1 Notre Dame for the BCS National Championship in Miami.

(Preceding page) Former UGA defensive back Kirby Smart was named head coach of the Bulldogs on Dec. 6, 2015. Photo by Sean Taylor. (Right) Mark Richt is one of the most beloved Georgia coaches ever. From 2001 through 2015 under Richt, the Dawgs had 145 wins and 51 losses. Photo by Steven Colquitt.

BULLDOGS

2007-2017

10 BIG GAMES REMEMBERED: 2007–2017

Sept. 22, 2007: Georgia 26, Alabama 23, OT, in Tuscaloosa. This was Nick Saban's initial year at Alabama, and Matthew Stafford's second at Georgia. The undefeated Tide scored 10 points in the fourth quarter to force the Bulldogs into overtime after they had taken a 20-10 lead. In OT, Alabama got the ball first and kicked a 42-yard field goal. On Georgia's first play, Stafford hit Mikey Henderson on a 25-yard pass for the win, a joyful occasion and something that would not be a common occurrence: Alabama losing a conference game at home.

"This was the national championship game," said many observers of the SEC final. The foregone conclusion was that the champion of the SEC would win the national title. Notre Dame made a game of it for a half in Miami, but Alabama won easily 42-14. Few would have advanced the notion that the Irish would have fared any better against the SEC runner-up.

Georgia's success ledger was impressive for much of the rest of Richt's career. He continued to win 10 games most seasons but there would be no championship. The criticism centered around UGA being a weak sister in a weak division, not playing tough enough on defense to win a title. The offense of coordinator Mike Bobo was graphically impressive, averaging 36.4 points per game his last four years; but to win a big game, the Bulldogs had to outscore opponents. They were often close but it became a challenge to win critical games that would move them into a championship opportunity.

■ RUNNING ON EMPTY WITH 11 WINS

The 2007 season was a study in a "what might have been" year. It was a good season, with 11 victories and a 41-10 thumping of Hawaii in the Sugar Bowl, but there were two telling warning signs: losing 16-12 to South Carolina at home, and getting whacked 35-14 in Knoxville.

After years of a busing via interstate highways 290 miles to Knoxville, roughly six hours, the Bulldogs now fly over the mountains, which is something like a 30-minute flight, and an easier road trip than a short bus ride to play Georgia Tech in Atlanta. But on Oct. 6, 2007, it was a depressing flight home. The Bulldogs did not "look good" in that SEC encounter, and realistically had no opportunity to compete for the SEC East — although they bested Florida 42-39 in Jacksonville and slammed Auburn 45-20 at home. It was too little too late, however. Finishing strong is always good for the emotions. The Dawgs beat

(Preceding page) Mikey Henderson (27) celebrates with his teammates after he caught a 25-yard touchdown pass from Matt Stafford to beat Alabama in 2007. Photo by Dean Legge.

Tech 31-7 between the hedges and had moved back into the BCS rankings after rolling over Hawaii in New Orleans. The final ranking was No. 2 in the AP poll, but there was an emptiness even with the good standing at the end.

When the 2010 season came around, there was grumbling about the Dawgs and their 8-5 record in 2009, although the team beat Tech and scored a half-dozen touchdowns in a 44-20 victory over Texas A&M in the Independence Bowl in Shreveport. But then the bottom would fall out in 2010, as Richt experienced his only losing season. Although he again won the state championship, frustration, carping and complaining set in as the Bulldogs lost 10-6 to Central Florida in the Liberty Bowl to conclude the season with a 6-7 record.

Back-to-back SEC East championship seasons in 2011 (10-4) and 2012 (12-2) were followed by teams that won eight to 10 games, but were missing a championship on the resume. The Bulldogs lost to Nebraska in the 2013 Taxslayer Gator Bowl but defeated Louisville 37-14 in the Belk Bowl in 2014 and Penn State 24-17 in the Gator Bowl in 2015.

In that latter bowl game, the head coach was Bryan McClendon, who like his father, Willie, was a successful player for the Bulldogs. By the time the bowl game came around, Athletics Director Greg McGarity had made a coaching change. The Mark Richt era, after 15 seasons, was over, following the Bulldogs' 13-7 defeat of Georgia Tech in Atlanta. Kirby Smart, who lettered for the Bulldogs as a defensive back from 1995-98, had been hired away from Alabama. (McClendon, at 1-0, nonetheless, became the fourth Georgia coach to post an undefeated record: Pop Warner, 4-0 in 1896; Herman Stegeman, 8-0-1 in 1920; Wallace Butts, 11-0 in 1946; and Vince Dooley 12-0 in 1980).

■ MARK RICHT: A DAMN GOOD DAWG

There were many highlights in the decade and a half Richt coached the Bulldogs. With a record of 145-51, he became the second winningest coach in Georgia history following Vince Dooley's 201-77-10. In terms of career winning percentage, Richt's is the best of all former Georgia head coaches.

Nov. 7, 2007: Georgia 45, Auburn 20, in Athens. Before the rivalry game "between the hedges," there was some scuttlebutt the Dawgs might don black jerseys. Coach Mark Richt was coy with everybody, but fans took the notion to heart, creating a "blackout" game. When the team came into the locker room from pregame warmups wearing the traditional red jerseys, Richt winked and said to me, "You might want to take cover. Something wild is about to happen." The players then noticed that in each locker there was a black jersey. Immediately, there was pandemonium as the overtly excited Bulldogs quickly removed their red jerseys and replaced them with black ones. It was a black-magic afternoon as Georgia turned a 20-17 third-quarter deficit into a 45-20 thrashing.

(Top left) Running back Knowshon Moreno bursts through a huge hole against Auburn in 2007. Photo by Radi Nabulsi. (Top right) Matt Stafford throws while on the run during 2007's victory over Auburn. Photo by Donavan Eason.

MATT STAFFORD:
The Bulldog With The Golden Arm

Years ago, quarterback Johnny Unitas became known as the man with the "Golden Arm" after his Baltimore Colts defeated the New York Giants at Yankee Stadium in the National Football League's first sudden-death championship game. That 23-17 victory on Dec. 28, 1958, has been called the "Greatest Game Ever Played," and Unitas has always been given the highest of marks for his role in the victory—propitious play calling, flawless execution and supreme confidence in what he was doing.

If he had been playing back then, Georgia's Matthew Stafford easily would have fit in with the "golden arms" of those days. It is doubtful that any arm of any Bulldog quarterback has ever been more golden than Stafford's.

Spud Chandler had to have had a fine arm in the late 1920s and early '30s. He is remembered for throwing a touchdown pass to Catfish Smith in the dedicatory game versus Yale, Oct. 12, 1929. He later became the MVP of the American League in 1943 while playing for the Yankees. His fastball brought him high praise and three World Series rings.

John Rauch had a good arm, his biggest asset being that he was keenly accurate. You probably could allow that Zeke Bratkowski, who ended up as the backup to Bart Starr with the Lombardi Packers, may have had the strongest arm of any Bulldog quarterback. You would have to give high marks to Larry Rakestraw, who had a versatile arm in that he could go deep and also had touch. Andy Johnson had arm strength, but was more recognized as a runner. Buck Belue will be remembered for winning a National Championship. Eric Zeier, who played six years with four teams in the NFL, had one of the most prolific arms in Georgia history. Quincy Carter, who wound up starting for the Dallas Cowboys for three seasons, certainly had arm strength but was conflicted by off-the-field distractions. Nobody could throw it deeper better than Jacob Eason, but he lacked in a couple of areas. This leaves us with a stirring omission: Fran Tarkenton, unquestionably was the most productive Bulldog quarterback ever. Fran once was a strong-arm QB pumping a football 70 yards downfield with ease. However, his high school coach, Weyman Sellers, a hardened disciple of Wallace Butts, never protected his quarterbacks—they had to do all the drills every other player was required to do! This included "head-on-tackling." When Sellers felt that the team played poorly one Friday night, he ordered up a full-scale scrimmage early Saturday morning. Tarkenton was the victim of a shoulder separation, following a no-holds-barred tackle. "My arm was never the same," Tarkenton says. "I lost at least 20 yards of distance." However, it was Fran who broke all of Johnny Unitas' records for total passes, competitions and career yards.

While there is always conjecture with any "superlatives" argument, it would be easy to conclude that the most golden of arms—arm strength, power, touch, flexibility (one who could make all the throws) and quick release—belonged to Stafford.

Stafford brought comparisons early on when he was a high school quarterback at Highland Park in Dallas to Bobby Layne, the legendary quarterback who preceded him at Highland Park and who, too, played with the Detroit Lions. Layne won three NFL titles at Detroit. A title is about the only thing missing on Stafford's resume, but he remains in the prime of life, so there is time for a Super Bowl championship.

Highly recruited, Stafford could have signed with any school, including Texas, where Layne also played. There was a Georgia connection in that his father, John, had enrolled in graduate school at Georgia and became an avid Bulldog fan. Greg Davis, who had coached the quarterbacks at Georgia in 1994-95, scouted Stafford and could not have been more bullish. Davis was the quarterback coach at Texas when Stafford was in high school and gave recruiting of Stafford to Austin the highest priority. He said, in a phone call after Matthew signed with Georgia: "He is the real deal, and one of the best I have ever seen." That Mike Bobo was the quarterback coach enhanced Stafford's decision. He liked Mark Richt, too, and he was compatible with Georgia's multiple offense.

Sometimes strong-armed quarterbacks have a weakness. They have so much confidence in their golden arms that they succumb to believing they can fire the ball into the tightest window. That can become a high-risk possibility or virtually impossible, which can lead to troublesome interceptions. Stafford was not immune to such circumstance. He knew he had exceptional arm strength, he believed in his golden arm.

There was no doubt about Stafford's tenure in Athens. He would be three and out. In his three years as a starter, he completed 564 of 987 pass attempts for a 57.1 completion percentage. He threw 51 touchdown passes against 33 interceptions for a rating of 133.3.

The Detroit Lions made him their first pick of the 2009 NFL Draft with the objective of building its team around one of the most talented quarterbacks to play between the hedges.

Photo by Donovan Eason.

UGA could not have had a more impressive and appreciated goodwill ambassador than Richt. He was a prolific speaker who would travel the state constantly to speak to church and charitable groups along with countless Bulldog Clubs.

He patterned his routine from the man he coached with for years, Bobby Bowden. Like Bowden, he was speaking somewhere almost every week, mostly to church groups. Richt became a beloved public figure in the state of Georgia and remains popular in the Peach State today.

His legacy will be that he put competitive teams on the field most years and gave the University of Georgia the most favorable image, a man of goodwill and fair play. He always competed by playing by the rules.

The Richt years were good years, and there was, for the most part, hopes that something spectacular would come about. Through it all, whatever success or disappointment, Richt remained the consummate nice guy. Georgia fans, even those who were blantly frustrated, took solace in the fact that Richt never embarrassed the university — and that he treated his players the way you would want your son to be treated.

Moving forward, this is not to analyze what the former coach didn't do — and let's not forget that he brought marked improvement when he took over in Athens in 2001 — it is about what was missing.

One day in the spring of 2005, best I recall, I was driving Richt through the Georgia campus to Ben Epps Field, the Athens municipal airport. We were taking a charter flight to a Bulldog Club meeting. It was a spring day for poets, just the most inspiring and resonating atmosphere you could imagine. Coeds sparkled in their sun dresses and you could feel the energy of the student body as we followed a stop-and-go routine resulting from pedestrian-clogged streets and walkways. You wanted the scene to last indefinitely instead of a few alacritous minutes.

Richt was taken by the glory of the moment and the beauty of the setting and said, "to mess this thing up, you would almost have to try." He and his family loved Athens and the environment. He long knew the potential that existed on the campus of the nation's oldest chartered state university.

During the signature days of Bobby Bowden's tenure at Florida State, the Seminole team spent its Friday nights in Thomasville, 34.2 miles from Tallahassee. Richt observed how competent high school football was in the state of Georgia. He read the *Thomasville Times* and regional papers and had a telling awareness that high school football in his neighboring state was important to the various populaces — which meant there were doting booster clubs that helped the local teams flourish.

The coaching in the state of Georgia was excellent, which was not lost on the FSU offensive coordinator. There were enough players in the state of Florida to keep the Seminoles a top 10 team nationally for years, but one example alone made Richt aware of the depth and talent in Georgia: Charlie Ward from Thomasville. Ward won the Heisman Trophy when Richt was at FSU.

The Thomasville Bulldogs had won state championships and fielded successful teams. Though Athens is 250 miles away, a lot of Thomasville players signed with the UGA Bulldogs. Some of that had to do with the fact that Georgia is the state university and the ties to Thomasville were strong and traditional. A significant influence was that Florida State began as a girls school and did not become competitive regionally or nationally until Bobby Bowden became established in the 1980s. Bill Peterson — the malapropos-waxing, ambitious, high-octane offense advocate of the passing game — was the FSU coach from 1960-70. Peterson brought the Seminoles some high moments, but it was Bowden who gave Leon County residents reason to puff out their chests.

Richt, who had played for Howard Schnellenberger at Miami, became quarterback coach at FSU in 1990 and the offensive coordinator in 1994. Bowden gave Richt high marks for his offensive creativity, noting that Richt's innovative embracing of no-huddle schemes was a major contribution to the ultra-offensive success FSU enjoyed.

However, this vignette may have forecast a forthcoming deficiency. When Georgia and Florida State met in the Sugar Bowl on Jan. 1, 2003, Vernon Brinson, a Georgia graduate who had played for Bowden at South Georgia Junior College in the late '50s, hosted a dinner at Commander's Palace, one of New Orleans'

Bulldog fans pack Sanford Stadium. Photo by University of Georgia Marketing & Communications.

BULLDOGS

Nose tackle Geno Atkins (56) sacks Hawaii quarterback Colt Brennan during the 2008 Sugar Bowl. Atkins was an Outland Trophy candidate at UGA before moving on to a stellar career in the NFL. Photo by Rebecca Hay.

10 BIG GAMES REMEMBERED: 2007–2017

Jan. 1, 2008: Georgia 41, Hawaii 10, in New Orleans. Mark Richt was bothered that his team, which had lost two games early but finished strong, was playing a Hawaii team that could get no respect. However, the Bulldogs scored early and often, and led 24-3 at the half. Knowshon Moreno and Thomas Brown had productive games, while the defense featured cornerback Asher Allen with nine tackles and two interceptions, and Sugar Bowl MVP Marcus Howard with three sacks — one of which created a fumble that Howard recovered in the end zone for a touchdown. Mark Richt really had nothing to worry about.

Moreno breaks loose against Hawaii in the Sugar Bowl. The second-team All-American finished his Georgia career with 2,734 rushing yards with 30 touchdowns, and 53 receptions for 645 yards and two scores. Photo by Rebecca Hay.

finest restaurants, for Bowden, a longtime assistant and friend, Vince Gibson and our wives. Bowden is the kind of guy who could enjoy a nice dinner with old friends, even those who would be pulling for his opponent on New Year's Day.

Bowden complimented Richt and his success with the Bulldogs winning the SEC Championship but offered this caveat: "I worried that he would not be tough enough." Then Bowden said warmly, "Looks like I was wrong and I am happy for him."

Richt's toughness, or perceived lack of it, would become a topic that Georgia fans debated and carped about in the end as the program continued to win games but struggled to win a championship after 2005.

In my relationship with him, I often would make comment about anything I felt that would be good for him to think about. I never second guessed his play calling or his coaching vagrancies — even with trusted friends. But it became evident the coach that got his players' attention the most was Brian VanGorder. VanGorder coached in Athens 2001-2004, and while the Bulldogs were able to win the SEC title in 2005 and had some good years thereafter, there was the inside view that VanGorder represented the toughness and measured discipline the team needed. Richt never replaced VanGorder in that sense, although, initially, Willie Martinez, who succeeded VanGorder as defensive coordinator, fielded defenses that averaged only three losses through 2008. Martinez left following the 2009 season.

With Matt Stafford coming along in 2006 and followed by Aaron Murray in 2010, there were notable highlights: 2007, when the Bulldogs were 11-2 and defeated Hawaii 41-10 in the Sugar Bowl; 2011, SEC East champions but lost badly 42-10 to LSU in the SEC title game; and, 2012, SEC East champions with a consequential 32-28 loss in the SEC title game to Alabama.

That last one was dejection squared and then some. Georgia was at the Alabama goal line with time running out. Score a touchdown and the Bulldogs play Notre Dame for the BCS National Championship. It was the opinion of most observers that whichever team won the SEC title would win the national title that year.

It was a sad moment for the coaches and staff, but you felt the most frustration of the loss for Aaron Murray, the game and gritty quarterback who gave his heart and soul to the Bulldogs and left everything on the field every time out.

After that, Richt would field winning teams, including 10-3 teams in 2014 and 2015, and two bowl games. In Richt's last season, he won nine games (10 if you want to suggest he would have won the Taxslayer Bowl), which brings forth the question of "Why was the Georgia hierarchy displeased?" Richt had only one losing season at Georgia and had coached his teams to 15 straight bowls.

Georgia's major donors — those who never go public, those who are loyal behind-the-scene supporters but weigh in at critical juncture — were of the view that while there was success, UGA was capable of winning championships, but that there had to be a change in leadership if titles were to be won in football in Athens.

The Mark Richt era, which many schools across the country would covet, was over. There were many who believed it was the right decision, but every one of them had nice things to say about the nice guy who had been the Bulldog coach. They knew he had represented the institution with class. They knew he had never embarrassed Georgia in any way. And they knew he had done his best to run a clean and honest program.

A new era had nonetheless, begun.

■ A SMART HIRE

"I don't think words can express how honored and privileged I am to stand before you as the head coach at the University of Georgia," Kirby Smart said at the press conference introducing him as Georgia's new head coach. "Our student-athletes will represent the university with class and integrity. We will demand that. Our teams will display great mental and physical toughness. We'll play with great confidence and pride on the field. We'll work toward this with relentless energy and passion, and I will demand that everyone in the organization does that."

There have been two dominant eras of Georgia football: the 1940s (compromised by World War II)

AARON MURRAY:
Admiring An Enduring Legacy

Aaron Murray was not exactly a heavyweight, but he wasn't a runt. He stood 6-foot-1 and weighed 207 pounds, most of that owing to his considerable heart. He loved football and he gave it his best every time out.

Georgia came up short in a couple of games with a championship in focus, but it wasn't because of a lack of leadership and effort on the part of their gritty quarterback, who was a gentleman and a competitor.

A native of Tampa, Aaron was a proponent of the "never give up" fraternity. He deserved better, principally in the 2012 SEC Championship Game when the Bulldogs came within one play of defeating Alabama and earning an opportunity to play No. 1 Notre Dame for the national title.

A good student and a community servant, Aaron was always helping others. Selfless and altruistic, he built a reputation of expansive goodwill in the community.

His leadership was critical to the success of the teams he played on at Georgia. He was intelligent and hard working. A team player, he started as a freshman and connected with his teammates. Following the leader became easy for his teammates.

In high school, he played in the shotgun formation his entire career, seldom if ever taking a snap from under center. He made the adjustment when he enrolled in Athens, owing to intelligence and sheer hard work.

When Aaron departed campus, he left a legacy that will endure. He will always be remembered and admired by the Bulldog Nation.

Photo by Wes Blankenship.

BULLDOG®

2007-2017

Linebacker Jarvis Jones (29), lineman DeAngelo Tyson (94) and the rest of the Bulldog defense shut down Florida's offense in the second half of 2011's victory over the Gators. Photo by John Kelley.

with Wallace Butts, and the early 1980s when Vince Dooley recruited Herschel Walker.

The notable overnight success by Smart in his first two years became a signal that a third era could possibly come about. Nobody is clairvoyant, however, and cynics have always preached "wait and see," but following the Dawgs' 2017 SEC title and the run to the College Football Playoff National Championship Game — and a subsequent recruiting windfall by Smart — had Georgia aficionados brimming with confidence that the leadership, work ethic and commitment based on cogent recruiting had at least put Georgia in a position to where it was realizing its full potential.

The SEC has been the best conference in college football the last two decades, led by Alabama with its five national titles since Nick Saban took over in Tuscaloosa. Georgia fans grew weary with Florida, LSU and Auburn being the only schools to break Alabama's stranglehold on the national title. While the Bulldogs remain hopeful, there is a growing confidence that Georgia can at least compete for the championship under Smart.

The fan base is confident their favorite team can segue from good to great. The man who has brought all this about says, "In football, nothing is guaranteed." You will never catch Kirby Smart saying anything inadvisable.

When Kirby officially returned Athens in December 2015, he found facilities lacking. The talent deficiency was already confirmed. He had evaluated Georgia's personnel from Alabama's 38-10 thrashing of the Bulldogs between the hedges in 2015. He knew Alabama's edge was far superior than what the most realistic Georgia aficionados would guess.

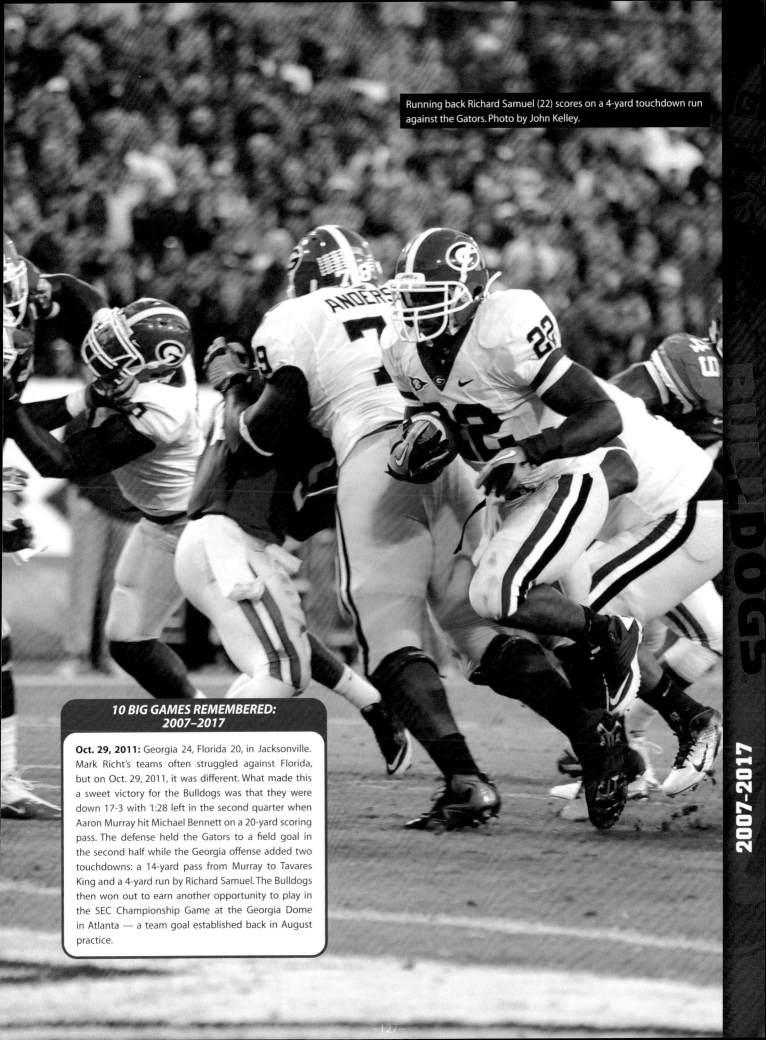

Running back Richard Samuel (22) scores on a 4-yard touchdown run against the Gators. Photo by John Kelley.

10 BIG GAMES REMEMBERED: 2007–2017

Oct. 29, 2011: Georgia 24, Florida 20, in Jacksonville. Mark Richt's teams often struggled against Florida, but on Oct. 29, 2011, it was different. What made this a sweet victory for the Bulldogs was that they were down 17-3 with 1:28 left in the second quarter when Aaron Murray hit Michael Bennett on a 20-yard scoring pass. The defense held the Gators to a field goal in the second half while the Georgia offense added two touchdowns: a 14-yard pass from Murray to Tavares King and a 4-yard run by Richard Samuel. The Bulldogs then won out to earn another opportunity to play in the SEC Championship Game at the Georgia Dome in Atlanta — a team goal established back in August practice.

KIRBY SMART:
A Homecoming Retrospective

It was a hot day, nauseatingly hot, when I stood on the practice field in the fall of 2017 and watched as the Georgia team was being cajoled, lectured, motivated and authenticated—a resounding litany of encouragement that only comes from a man on a mission.

Kirby Smart has been that man on a mission since he was named Georgia's head coach Dec. 6, 2015.

It was a signature moment when the former UGA defensive back was hired by Athletics Director Greg McGarity to become Georgia's 28th head coach. He is one of six undergraduates who have enjoyed the honor of becoming the UGA football boss: Charles Herty, M.M. Dickinson, Kid Woodruff, Johnny Griffith and Ray Goff.

Something singular developed early on in his tenure. He is a first-name Bulldog personality. Dating back, head football coaches have traditionally been identified with title and surname: Coach Mehre, Coach Butts, Coach Dooley. With the current director of football at UGA, it is simply "Kirby." With his competency and promise, Kirby could become another icon whose first name dominates, as in Herschel rather than Herschel Walker.

To assess Kirby's budding career, you learn from looking into his past that there is a significant coaching pedigree. His father, Sonny Smart, coached Kirby at Bainbridge in southwest Georgia. Sonny never yearned for his son to follow in his footsteps, and now that Kirby has reached exalted status as a coach at a major university in the most dominant league in college football the last 20 years, he will not relive his life through his son. Sonny is happily ensconced in the background. There is no coaching from the sideline in this family, but if Kirby wants advice when it comes to serious football matters, he knows where to turn. Sonny's ambition for Kirby is as keen as Kirby's when it comes to aspiring for championship success to become the focal point of the Kirby Smart legacy.

In addition to growing up in a coaching household that allowed for a close-up view of how football must become family—like family at home—Kirby, by absorption, learned about the immaturity of youth and how it affects a team. He became familiar with the mores of the times and the significance of discipline, noting that kids react differently to motivation overtures. There is one uncompromising staple: If there is success, you must pay the price, and everybody must buy in to the larger objectives of the team.

Most of all, no coach has ever prepared himself better to become a head coach. When he was waiting in the wings, Kirby learned the value of patience. He didn't jump at any job. While he did not have a grand scheme to return to his alma mater, he knew what he wanted in becoming a head coach. Georgia fit all the criteria. He evaluated other schools, other programs, other coaches—but most of all, he was learning about how an elite program is managed while apprenticing under the most successful coach in the land in Nick Saban. Kirby lived success with Saban, and formulated a plan and philosophy which is, understandably, devoutly Sabanese. However, he will tell you that he has approached his life as the head Bulldog by "being his own man." He is aware that iconic coaches, more often than not, spawn failed coaching careers.

Kirby's respect for Saban is lofty and abiding. "The most valuable thing I learned is how to run an organization from top to bottom; being demanding of people in the organization and expecting that they all perform at a certain level and a certain standard, making them realize that standard does not change based on whether you win or lose. He is head and shoulders above the others because of his management style and passion. The guy is relentless. He works his tail off."

That it worked out for him to return to Athens, where in addition to playing with the Dawgs, he was an assistant briefly (running backs in 2005), brings about warm sentiment. He knows his alma mater offers championship opportunity and that not to win championships would be underachieving. He knows what it takes to win.

At Alabama, when Kirby reviewed game tape of opponents, he saw which teams were the best coached, those which underscored teaching, discipline and were imbued to

commitment to fundamentals. Long before "Mama called," he had a general idea of who the best assistants in the conference were. He had a potential staff conjured up in his head while he was working to improve himself as a defensive coordinator in Tuscaloosa.

He is a Georgia boy with a Georgia education. Nothing finer, the late Dean of Men, William Tate, said about that. Everything is in place for a bountiful career. He has feeling and respect for his past. He loves Bainbridge and South Georgia from whence he came. He loves his native state and connects with every county through recruiting.

Love of alma mater is deep and resonating. Early on, he became a Bulldog fan, but in his formative years he was all about "Friday Night Lights." His heroes all played for the Bainbridge Bearcats. His time was the late '80s, following the Herschel era. Signed by Ray Goff, Kirby lettered four years (1995-98) and was elected a defensive captain his senior season, evidence that his ability to lead was manifesting itself. His coach for three seasons, Jim Donnan says, "Kirby was a coach on the field for our defense besides being a very good athlete at free safety."

There were highlights as a Bulldog safety, including making three sacks against South Carolina between the hedges in 1995 and two interceptions in the Florida game in 1997 in a 37-17 Bulldog victory. At Georgia, there were no championships during his career, but three bowl games and countless friendships that have endured. Throughout his coaching career he has kept in touch with his old friends.

Any story about his college years without reference to his Terry College degree would make the story incomplete. He is proud of the degree, naturally. An offspring of teachers (he still hears his mother, Sharon, reminding him to read more books), who have always influenced him to embrace the importance of school work, has brought about a residual as a coach. He passionately explains to the players he recruits that a degree is not only important, but is achievable by underscoring the same basics that enables success to come about on the field— it all begins with discipline and hard work.

One of his teammates, Dax Langley, who was a placekicker and now an Athens businessman, offers the highest praise. "Kirby," he says, "has not changed one bit. He is the same today as he was when he was a raw freshman. His priorities were in order then, just as they are now. A good example of that was that he gave the same effort as a student as he did as a player. If he had homework to do, he would stay away from a fraternity party until he had done his homework."

Those who know him best would conclude that he has a coach's mindset, the ultimate due diligent advocate who is always prepared and considers all the angles. Fueled by a dedicated work ethic, enhanced by perpetual enthusiasm and seasoned judgment, his courtship with Mary Beth Lycett confirms the above is ever present in his makeup.

When she was being recruited by Andy Landers out of Morrow High School, she remembers seeing Kirby play between the hedges, Nov. 15, 1997. On that bitterly cold day, she had no idea who wore No. 16 or what he did on that field when the Bulldog defense was being overwhelmed by giving up 45 points to Auburn. You have to fast forward to learn how they became permanently linked. They became acquainted

when she joined the business office of the Athletic Association after graduation, and he showed up to coach the Bulldog running backs. He "checked her out" by doing his own scouting report by consulting with the Lady Dawg basketball staff.

When asked about Kirby, she comes forth with a laudable and reverential assessment. "I just don't see how anybody could work any harder than he does. Still, he finds time for family. He is really honest with everybody. He is that way with me and the kids. There is not a lot of time for us, understandably, during the season and that stretches right on into recruiting. He is passionate about recruiting as he is about anything. He knows recruiting is where success begins.

"Even so, I have seen him during his busiest time stay on the phone trying to help friends in coaching with their job search," she continued. "He reaches out on their behalf. His friends are really important to him. That is why he has kept in touch with his buddies from his Georgia days.

"Kirby dotes on our kids (twins Weston and Julia, and Andrew) and a highlight of the year is when he takes the family snow skiing after recruiting is over."

On coming back "home," Mary Beth, who was a four-year letterwinner and a two year starter for the Lady Dawg basketball team, found the situation surreal. "He had turned down other opportunities, wanting to make sure that he made the best decision—trying to make sure he waited for the right job—but we never planned for it to be Georgia. That it worked out has made us very, very happy."

Having competed on the college level, she considers that an asset which enables her to understand the rigors of being a head coach who has to endure stress and pressure and the vicissitudes in the life of today's celebrated athletes whose heads are easily turned with the fame and potential fortune that surrounds them.

Kirby's office reveals that he is a busy man, with neat stacks of papers arranged to accommodate his requirements for the day. There are artifacts of his playing and coaching careers: photo art of him huddling with his teammates at Sanford Stadium, family photos, a couple of Steve Penley paintings (in his outer office), a game ball from an Alabama CFP playoff victory, and a photo of him and his parents on Senior Day when he would play his last game in Sanford Stadium. But most prominent is his framed diploma from the Terry College of Business. There is also his diploma from Florida State, where he earned a Master's degree as a graduate assistant member of Bobby Bowden's staff, and his trophy as winner of the 2009 Broyles Award for Assistant Coach of the Year.

Outside his office is a photo display of his signature accomplishments (four-time national champion, five-time SEC champion, seven-time SEC divisional champion) and an action photo of Mary Beth in her Lady Dawg uniform. A loyal Bulldog and Georgia graduate, he is very proud of his wife being a letterwinner at his alma mater.

All this reflects accomplishment and the right fit to take Georgia to a consistent championship level. He never takes things for granted, however. Always reaching for the prize, he is comfortable with the expectations that hover around him. No Bulldog of any status expects more of Kirby Smart than Kirby Smart himself.

To begin with, he had to change the culture. Georgia had no killer instinct. The Bulldogs couldn't close. The team that couldn't finish the drill was the team that came up with that slogan.

The shortcoming in attitude was confirmed for this Georgia alumnus in the Florida game Kirby's first year. I no longer hang out on the sideline during games, but I went down in the fourth quarter when Florida put together a two-touchdown lead. While it would have taken a favorable sequence of events for Georgia to have won the game, think about it: score, get a break, gain the momentum and it certainly was possible. The team had the look of sleepwalkers, save one: Mo Smith, the defensive back who chose to play his last year at Georgia, was dog-cussing his teammates, exhorting them with a vernacular they understood. "Don't you guys want to win?" he shouted, tossing about expletives like a boatswain's mate.

Even though this was a team that did not have the players to compete for a championship and had not been disciplined with an edge, it might have been more successful with the right attitude. While pointing fingers is an exercise in futility, I will maintain that his inherited team let him down. Mostly, the team needed an attitude adjustment.

No team with ingrained discipline has a player run on the field with his helmet off to join what should have been a victory celebration versus Tennessee in 2016. Yet, the new head coach did not throw him under the bus. I'm not sure what took place privately, but it became apparent that it was addressed.

It didn't take long for most partisans and observers to see that the head coach — a play-action, hard-nosed defensive advocate — would find a way to give his team the edge. This "Smart coach" will never beat himself with his mouth.

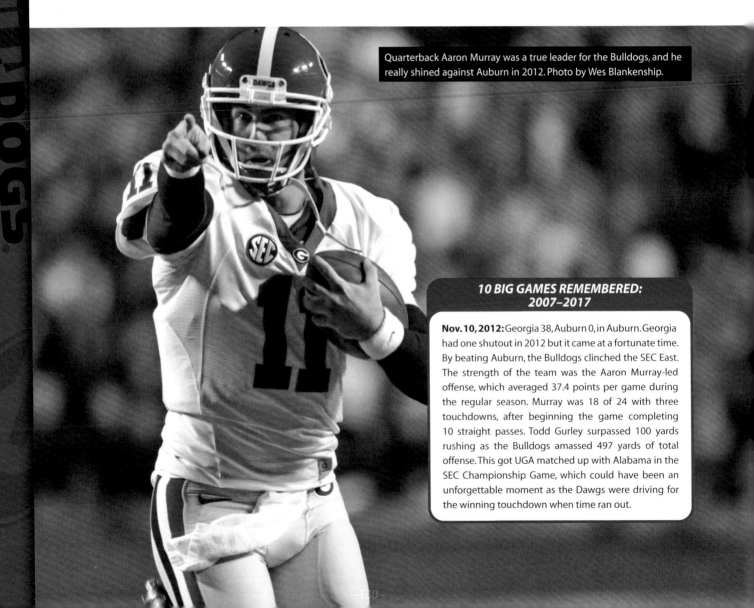

Quarterback Aaron Murray was a true leader for the Bulldogs, and he really shined against Auburn in 2012. Photo by Wes Blankenship.

10 BIG GAMES REMEMBERED: 2007–2017

Nov. 10, 2012: Georgia 38, Auburn 0, in Auburn. Georgia had one shutout in 2012 but it came at a fortunate time. By beating Auburn, the Bulldogs clinched the SEC East. The strength of the team was the Aaron Murray-led offense, which averaged 37.4 points per game during the regular season. Murray was 18 of 24 with three touchdowns, after beginning the game completing 10 straight passes. Todd Gurley surpassed 100 yards rushing as the Bulldogs amassed 497 yards of total offense. This got UGA matched up with Alabama in the SEC Championship Game, which could have been an unforgettable moment as the Dawgs were driving for the winning touchdown when time ran out.

If you play for Kirby, you not only refrain from stomping on your opponent's logo, you don't even think about it. He is a "say nice things about your opponent" proponent. You'll never hear him criticize an opposing coach, even in private. On top of that, there is no place for trash-talking your opponent. It can always come back to haunt you. This insight confirms that he is a coach who considers little things unceasingly important.

■ TURNING IT AROUND QUICKLY

It is doubtful anyone familiar with the Georgia scene, and college football in general, predicted the serendipitous season of 2017, the Dawgs coming within one play of winning the national title — one defensive stop, one first down, one less officiating faux pas against Saban's Crimson Tide.

But on the other hand, why should Smart not have turned things around overnight in Athens? Even in his first year, he confirmed he is a consequential salesman. Recruiting was not top drawer like it was in 2017 and off the charts like it would be in 2018, but it was much improved.

If he and his staff could sell precocious recruits to fill their wardrobes with red and black, why couldn't they convince incumbents on buying into the process that would bring about a consistency of winning with a focus on championships? All Georgia fans had to do was to exercise patience.

Kirby Smart has been a man on a mission since he held his first press conference as Georgia's coach, even with bitter disappointment engulfing him in the first offseason after his first year. "Eight and five," he said with disgust. Downright contempt for results, but he never threw his dysfunctional team under the bus.

You see him rant and rave at practice, which is a teaching exercise, cramming a PhD workload into 120 minutes. (The rules allow no more, but the rules can't dictate his personal commitment, which is roughly 80 hours a week.) He will kick ass, but he is mostly a teacher, a leader. He is not an enforcer, yet he rigidly enforces his rules. He understands today's youth, and he understands what works when it comes to team building. He had to change the culture before success ensued.

Success begets success. A year after "Doubting Thomases," the unwashed, allowed sour grapes to set their critical tongues to waging, the "Serendipity Dawgs" blossomed into a contender, and then a champion. They stubbed their toe only once but were able to rebound and win twice more before heartbreak robbed them of the ultimate ecstasy. They felt they should have won it all, but truth of the matter, Kirby got Georgia to the "promised land" ahead of schedule. Conventional wisdom suggests you need superb back-to-back-to-back recruiting classes to move into the College Football Playoff. Kirby got the Dawgs there in two.

There were so many turning points since the former Georgia defensive back returned home to run his alma mater's football program: flipping the commitment of Jake Fromm from Alabama to Georgia; the recruiting of Nick Chubb, Sony Michel, Lorenzo Carter and Davin Bellamy away from the NFL; the maturation of the offensive line; the scintillating play of Roquan Smith, the most exciting linebacker to wear the red and black.

It is the players who count. That view has been espoused since the days of Walter Camp, and we know it is unalterably true that you can't "win without he hosses." However, the man most responsible for the glory that came ol' Georgia's way was the "Smart" man in charge.

He has the moxie, the savvy and the competitive sense to bring the ultimate achievement to the hallowed hedges. I like it that his teams are opportunistic and well disciplined. I like it that his first priority is recruiting. I like it that you won't hear him make an ill-advised statement about any shortcoming on the scoreboard. I like it that he accentuates positive. I like it that you won't see a player of his spiking an opponent's logo. I like it when he tells his team never to rub it in. "Men," he will say, "We gotta play these guys next year."

I am a Kirby man. Nobody's clairvoyant, but the seasoned view here is that as time moves on, to beat Georgia, you got to beat the Bulldog coach. That is gonna be hard to do.

MEL TUCKER:
"Few SEC Towns Have What Athens Has"

Mel Tucker likes good scotch, the high-end stuff like, "The Macallan," and I like buying him good scotch. He makes a lot more money than I do, but he works for my alma mater, expertly coaching Bulldog defenders to "hold that line." That justifies my investment in our friendship.

There is a downside with our friendship, however. He spends so much time grinding away at the office that it is difficult to socialize with him. Whenever I do, I come away with an appreciation for his football insights, which are such that somebody will soon take him from us. He is destined to be a head coach.

That time will bring about a Shakespearean reflection. "Parting will be such sweet sorrow." But let's not give anybody any ideas. For the moment, let's settle in with him and his memories of 2017, preceded by a reflection into his past when he chose a path that moved him to the head of the defensive coaching class.

A suburban kid who was influenced by outdoors, he has a degree in agricultural business management (1995) from Wisconsin, where he lettered for four years under Barry Alvarez. Mel is a man of varied interests—a polymath with an inquiring mind. He is an aficionado of gadgets, which he collects—motivated to see how things work, an inspiration that translates into cogent defensive scheming. Yet, he can be attracted to the simplest of things, such as collecting trading cards growing up and playing the fiddle (the better the scotch, the better he plays).

There was familial emphasis growing up. His father, Mel Sr., was a tight end who was coached by former Georgia receivers coach Bob Harrison. The senior Tucker developed a head-turning resume at Toledo where he was inducted into the Rockets Hall of Fame. Daddy-coach taught Mel the rudiments of the quarterback option. And like father like son, it was football in the fall, basketball in the winter, and baseball in the spring.

The elder Tucker influenced his son to appreciate the hometown team. As often as possible, they witnessed the action first hand, experiencing the on-the-field (or on-the-court) vicissitudes of the Browns, Indians and Cavaliers. Growing up in Cleveland, there was no place Mel would rather be than the Dawg Pound on Sunday afternoon. He thrilled to NFL flashbacks of the gliding rushing style and staccato bursts of incomparable running back Jim Brown, never thinking for an instant he would later became friends with this iconic football hero.

While football is his profession, Mel has an inclination for a well-rounded lifestyle and can enjoy an evening of conversion that touches on more than the nuances of the 3-4 defense. As he savors his Macallan, he lets you in on a secret he knows about the arts and cultural goings-on at UGA: "What other SEC school," he asks, "has a symphony?"

Fresh out of Wisconsin, he joined Nick Saban's Michigan State staff in 1997 as a graduate assistant, the beginning of a football coaching odyssey that brought about a mix of professional and collegiate exposure: Miami of Ohio, Ohio State, Cleveland Browns, Jacksonville Jaguars, Chicago Bears and Alabama. At 29, he was the co-defensive coordinator at Ohio State; at 36, he became the defensive coordinator of the hometown Browns, a responsibility he also held with the Jaguars and the Bears before rejoining Saban as the defensive backfield coach at Alabama, where he developed a friendship with Kirby Smart.

With his exposure to coaching opportunities, Mel is the beneficiary of "local" knowledge, which coupled with scuttlebutt in the profession, made him aware of the compelling potential that defines opportunity at the University of Georgia. A friend who played at Tennessee holds the view that the Georgia job is the "best in the country."

After time spent in Athens, Mel endorses the notion that while UGA is a special place, the key to success "is signing the right players." Georgia compares favorably with schools like Ohio State, LSU, Nebraska and Wisconsin in that those institutions are the only major college in that state. "We, of course," he says, "cannot overlook Georgia Tech, which has a great tradition and has enjoyed great success. "Few SEC towns have what Athens has—a hardcore football commitment with progressive energy and a hungry-to-win atmosphere. There is enterprising enlightenment here," Mel says.

Photo by Steven Colquitt

■ THE EASON FACTOR

In 2017, nobody expected the Bulldogs to stir the SEC pot, especially when the heralded sophomore quarterback, Jacob Eason, was injured in the first quarter of the season opener against Appalachian State. It was an untimely shot out of bounds by defensive end Myquon Stouton, a blow to Eason's left knee. The Georgia quarterback got up slowly and walked back to the huddle, where he collapsed. Not only was he done for the game, he was essentially done for the season.

The offensive coaches had planned to play precocious freshman backup Jake Fromm as much as they could in that they believed in him and expected to be prepared for such an eventuality. However, they didn't expect it to come so quickly.

With Eason, there is a vignette that brings forth a worthy insight. It was his recruitment, and his classy handling of a sensitive and disappointing situation. The fact that he moved to the opposite coast to ply his quarterbacking trade tells you the previous staff did a fine job recruiting him, and secondly, it tells you more that he passionately connected to the Georgia campus. His parents, Tony and Christine, fell in love with UGA as well. When misfortune came his way, Jacob handled it like an All-American. He didn't carp, he didn't complain, and he didn't become a sorehead. He got to play in mop-up roles, which was tough on his ego. Eason's commitment to being a team player was a significant factor in Georgia's success.

You won't find a Georgia coach who doesn't think Eason won't be a fixture in the NFL. However, it is easy to conclude, he is not a play-action quarterback. Jake Fromm is.

Fromm was suddenly inserted into the lineup in the first game, the greenest of quarterbacks since David Greene took over during Richt's first season, but Greene had a redshirt year of valuable experience. Fromm immediately acquitted himself well, which did not surprise the Georgia coaches. He was comfortable in the huddle.

The videotape machine became Fromm's daily partner. He was an eager and devout student of the game, but that had been the case with him historically. He ran Georgia's play-action offense, which got better and better as the offensive line got better and better, superbly.

With Fromm's cogent improvement, there was, nonetheless, an undercurrent of concern. The coaches wanted Eason to become healthy again. What if some defender hit Fromm out of bounds late? The team could experience a negative déjà vu moment, experiencing the same situation in reverse.

In time, Fromm would become an intellectual leader and compelling performer. Offensive coordinator Jim Chaney would allow more independence when it came to play-calling. By the end of the season, the young man had earned Chaney's confidence to the point that he was allowed to counter Chaney's calls.

Justin Scott-Wesley scored what would be the game-winning touchdown against LSU in 2013. Photo by John Kelley.

> ### 10 BIG GAMES REMEMBERED: 2007–2017
>
> **Sept. 28, 2013:** Georgia 44, LSU 41, in Athens. No. 9 Georgia had a hot quarterback when No. 6 LSU came to town, but so did the Tigers, as it was a faceoff of former teammates Aaron Murray and Zach Mettenberger. The rivals for the UGA starting position became rivals in one of the most exciting games ever played between the hedges, which were ringed with 92,746 doting fans. With LSU leading 41-37, Murray drove the Bulldogs 75 yards in six plays, completing a pass to Justin Scott-Wesley for a 44-41 lead with 1:47 left. Mettenberger could still be the hero, but four consecutive incompletions, as the Georgia defense suddenly was at its best in 2013, enabled the Dawgs to finish the drill.

ROQUAN SMITH:
A Heart Bent Toward Extraordinary Performance

There are approximately 1,335 residents in Marshallville, Georgia, and from Roquan Smith's perspective, "all of them are Dawg fans, except for those who might not ever have heard of Athens." Marshallville is the hometown of the Georgia All-America linebacker who was schooled in the Macon County system, 14 miles away in Montezuma.

Roquan grew up near the Flint River, where he learned to swim and fish. His life, as it is for so many in his "neck of the woods," was laid back and uncomplicated. There were a lot of backyard games with family, friends and neighbors. He learned about competition early on. Kids, especially those in semi-rural settings, often are affected by austerity when it comes to facilities and sporting equipment.

They have to be inventive. Roquan and his friends played a game called "Throw 'em up, bust 'em up." Everybody gathers into a tight circle. The one in the center has a ball and tosses it in the air, like the opening tipoff in basketball. Everybody fights for the ball and the one who gains possession throws it up, and the fight for possession continues until somebody eventually scores.

That is where Roquan got his first taste of gang tackling "I loved the contact, I loved the fight for the ball," he said with a smile when recalling his growing-up days in Marshallville.

When Roquan returns home, his life flips upside down. Everyone wants to shake his hand. They want to talk football with him and get his take on Chicago, which became his NFL home following his consequential years as a Bulldog.

Marshallville didn't have a football program, and early on, Roquan was a fit for the game. First of all, he had good feet, which complimented his football sense of direction. You are at top speed moving in one direction and suddenly you have to pivot and go in the opposite direction. The defender doesn't know where the ball carrier is going. Roquan's football instincts, however, allowed him to anticipate adroitly and meet up with the ball carrier with propitious timing. Short-yardage gains, no gains and, the most fulfilling of statistics for a linebacker, the acronym TFL.

A tackle-for-loss is a football defender's watershed moment. It is the defensive equivalent of a run for a first down. Or a touchdown. In certain circumstances, it could carry greater impact. It could interrupt or stop a drive that left unchecked might result in points scored. It could force a would-be-touchdown into a field-goal attempt. It could take the offense out of field-goal range. TFLs don't bring the attention that a running back gets when he bolts past the line of scrimmage and runs to daylight all the way to the opponent's end zone, but in terms of winning, those defensive plays are just as important as yardage-gulping plays on offense.

Roquan's agility and sense of where the ball is, his recognition and reaction instincts were a natural gift, but nobody worked harder than this Marshallvillian to hone his skills into defensive competency that brought about All-America honors. The last player to have made All-America at Georgia was Jarvis Jones in 2012.

But most importantly, Roquan always had his game face on. Throughout the season, he was like a stealth imbued panther, always ready to pounce at every opportunity. He was always engaged, cogently prepared and keen on being in the right place at the right time. If he were a gambler, winner take all would be his game.

With a heart bent toward extraordinary performance — giving of himself for the team — Roquan, the lionhearted, rendered performances his last season as a Bulldog that confirm why he was chosen All-America. A game in which he could be seen "all over the field" was the regular-season finale. The Georgia defense lined him up head-on center. Wherever the ball went, Roquan went. Right or left, didn't matter. He may not have been the first defensive center-fielder, but nobody has ever wreaked more havoc. He had nine defense stops, which included three TFLs and a sack. "That was a very rewarding game," he said. "I like to talk about that game because our defense was so dominating." z The next highlight came in the rematch with Auburn: 13 tackles, a sack, one TFL and two fumble recoveries. He was named the MVP. The team knew that winning the SEC title would get the Bulldogs into the College Football Playoff — and nobody was more primed for influencing the outcome than Roquan Smith.

In Macon County, emotions were over the top for the populace. One of its own had helped make it happen.

Now they wait to see if he can enjoy championship success at the next level. Those who know him would not be surprised. For sure, the Dawg fans in Marshallville and Montezuma are anxious for the next chapter in his life.

■ 2017'S SURPRISE RISE

However, all hands on deck were nervous as hell for the Notre Dame game at South Bend on Sept. 9, 2017. Starting a rookie quarterback against a team that represented, perhaps, the most storied programs in collegiate football history! Kirby Smart would be coaching on the same field where Rockne, Leahy, Parseghian and Holtz coached. Fromm would trod the turf of Gipp, Lujack, Hornung and Montana, among others.

At that point in the season, Georgia was green but growing. Notre Dame was rebounding from a disappointing season in 2016 with an enduring pre-season commitment for pronounced improvement. It would be a tough game. Notre Dame had a viable and experienced quarterback, and the Irish expected themselves to perform better than the visitors in full view of Touchdown Jesus.

(Above right) Running back Sony Michel eyes a hole in the Notre Dame defensive line. Photo by Perry McIntyre. (Below right) With two minutes remaining against Notre Dame in 2017, Davin Bellamy (17) sacks the Irish quarterback, forcing a fumble that Lorenzo Carter recovered to ice the victory. Photo by Perry McIntyre.

10 BIG GAMES REMEMBERED: 2007–2017

Sept. 9, 2017: Georgia 20, Notre Dame 19, in South Bend. It was a phantasmagorical moment, dreamlike, for both the fans and team. Precocious freshman quarterback Jake Fromm would be starting for the first time, in a shrine. With the Bulldog offensive line, it was still on-the-job training. The defense played at a peak with propitious timing, like with two minutes left when Davin Bellamy sacked the Irish quarterback, forcing a fumble that Lorenzo Carter recovered. High marks were in order for Rodrigo Blankenship, who kicked the winning field goal, and Terry Godwin's one-handed scoring catch at the back-corner pylon — which "further review" overturned the on-the-field decision that the catch was incomplete.

NICK & SONY:
The Best Of Friends

The story that has prevailed over the years is that Roger Maris and Mickey Mantle were the best of friends and that there was no rivalry between them when they were bashing their way to American League home run titles in the late 1950s and early '60s.

It was said that Mickey was one of Roger's biggest cheerleaders when the latter was about to set a single-season home run record in 1961, the year Maris broke Babe Ruth's mark of 60 homers in a season.

In Athens, it was the same with Frank Sinkwich and Charley Trippi in the same backfield. That role existed for only a few games, but it is obvious there has ever been a more potent offensive running back combination at Georgia until Nick Chubb and Sony Michel peaked in 2017, just like Sinkwich and Trippi in 1942.

There was Koufax and Drysdale with the Dodgers, Jordan and Pippen with the Bulls, the Lone Ranger and Tonto, Rhett Butler and Scarlett O'Hara, and Simon and Garfunkel — all classic duos, but for friendship, fellowship, harmony and productivity, who could have overwhelmed more than Nick and Sony?

A selfless attitude, that love for one another, does make a difference when it comes to team bonding and competing for the big prize.

Nick and Sony first met at an all-star game when they both were committed to enroll at the University of Georgia. The mutual admiration society took root early on. Eventually, they would become best friends and roommates. As the 2016 season was sliding into the past, the two most productive running backs in Georgia history, during a lull in their room one day, decided they were going to return to UGA for their final year of eligibility. It was a telling moment when they hit upon the thought simultaneously that they wanted to forgo the NFL Draft in 2017 so they could take care of unfinished business in Athens.

When they told coach Kirby Smart, he almost lost his measured, unemotional style; his cool collapsed when the supercalifragilistic moment sallied forth.

The litany of sidebars to their head-turning selfless relationship is innumerable, and the times when each gave way to the other when underscoring the importance of team play are countless. It makes you reflect on that slogan of the '80 championship season, "BIG" team, Little "me." No two players have ever been greater team aficionado's than this pair.

"We compete with great passion to be the best — to make the team better," Nick says.

Sony's comment is as if their attitudes were scripted. "We push each other hard so that it helps the team."

Neither has a scrapbook. Neither likes the interview process for one reflective reason: they don't like to talk about themselves. Nobody has ever championed the love of teammates more than Nick and Sony.

The first brick in the foundation to the 2017 SEC Championship season was confirmation that the two running backs would return for their senior season. When their teammates saw them in perfect harmony, it made the rest of the team realize that championships only come about when there is selfless leadership at the top. Nick and Sony personified selflessness from the start.

A TRIP TO CHUBBTOWN

In the summer before Nick's sophomore season, I had a conversation with his father, Henry, in Chubbtown. "Right now," he said, "I believe that Nick will stay four years at Georgia." I had spent the afternoon with Henry, starting out in Cedartown, where Nicholas (the family never refers to him as Nick) grew up, with an agenda to learn about the history of Chubbtown, which has now been chronicled and reported on constantly since the story got out about the original eight brothers who migrated from the Virginia/North Carolina line to West Georgia. Nicholas is named for one of the "original" Chubbs.

As a kid, Nick was the traditional every-sport participant, but not taking to baseball because there was "too much standing around. I wanted to run." He often lined up against his brother in the yard at home, a one-on-one competition to see who could outmaneuver or who could stop the other. He knows the history of Chubbtown and still enjoys returning to the little white church where he once served as an altar boy.

Nick stays away from parties, and while not unfriendly, he prefers private time. On the Rose Bowl trip while some of his teammates were soaking up the atmosphere of Los Angeles, he often would take to his room and sleep. He wanted to be relaxed and ready, fresh and with a keen edge when the game started.

Now that NFL paydays are here, what will Nick Chubb do when it comes time to settle down for the rest of his life? He would like to own a small farm in Polk County. This is a young man who will be exposed to the sights and sounds of the biggest cities and stadiums in the country. When there is down time, when he can get away, it will be to enjoy the enrichment of the simple life where he grew up.

FROM HAITI TO ATHENS

Sony Michel is from the islands. His family sought to emigrate from Haiti to South Florida for a better life. His parents still speak Creole, which was the language he was first exposed to in his early years as a child, but English is his first language.

Sony's sport in those formative years was soccer, but he took to football like a duck to water. When his family settled down in Florida and was introduced to football, he was immediately smitten. Neighborhood games were the order of the day. Tackle in the street in street clothes toughened him up right away, and he left a legacy for hard work when he moved on to the University of Georgia from American Heritage High School in Plantation, near Fort Lauderdale.

Following the end of Georgia's 2017 SEC Championship season, Sony (like his buddy Nick) chose to prepare for the NFL Draft by returning home for a pre-draft training program. It was an early-to-bed, early-to-rise routine that began on the beach at sunup, running and doing agility drills in the sand. Then there was weightlifting and other drills that would have Sony in peak condition by the time he got to the NFL Scouting Combine in Indianapolis.

Respect for the work ethic was handed down from his parents who allowed him to pursue his abiding interest in sports. He "worked" at sports from grade school through high school graduation and beyond. With that luxury, he took advantage by being grateful, diligent and forthright. He set his sights on being the best he could be.

On returning for one more year, he "felt like I had more to give to Georgia." With a semester left, he will concentrate on completing degree requirements in communication. That will bring about a high moment. "That is why you go to college, to get a degree, and I am committed to doing that."

He has not given much thought to the fact that his performance in Pasadena puts him in the pantheon of Bulldog greatness. But to score the tying and winning touchdowns on the Rose Bowl stage and get Georgia into the National Championship Game will be a memorable highlight that will live in redundancy. His mad-dog dash to the end zone to win the Rose Bowl will have an everlasting impact for generations. Even as we speak, somebody, somewhere, is watching a replay of that touchdown on their iPhone.

It is on Sony's iPhone, too, as a keepsake but he seldom watches it. Someday he expects to have a home with a memory nook featuring that run. "I am sure it will mean more to me as I get older," he says.

No Georgia bowl game has ever had a more sensational finish, and it will long be remembered as a classic performance that featured one of the greatest plays in Georgia football history.

UNTIL WE MEET AGAIN

The last public appearance of Sony (No. 1) and Nick (No. 27) came at the spring game in April 2018, which came close to being a sellout. The friends showed up, each in the other's jersey: Nick wore No. 1 and Sony wore No. 27. Whose idea was that? They responded with "Both of us." What would one expect?

Soon after the spring game the duo became early NFL Draft picks, Sony to the New England Patriots in the first round and Nick to the Cleveland Browns early in the second. Their brotherly love, mutual admiration society will be splintered as they go their separate ways, but nonetheless, they expect to maintain an abiding friendship the rest of their lives.

Sony Michel (1) and Nick Chubb (27) lining up against Appalachian State in 2017. Photo by Caitlyn Tam.

Fromm had some freshman moments, but he also sparked some heady plays to keep the Bulldogs in the game. Terry Godwin's remarkable touchdown catch in the second quarter was one of the most spectacular in history, akin to the ones authored by A.J. Green. It would come down to Rodrigo Blankenship's 30-yard field goal, opportunity brought about with defensive tenacity and seasoned offensive thrusts by running backs Nick Chubb and Sony Michel.

"Men," said a drained Smart after the game, "that's a fine football team you beat tonight." He subsequently and enthusiastically complimented his entire team, as he is wont to do, and then asked Blankenship,

(Below) Running back Nick Chubb takes off against Auburn in the 2017 SEC Championship Game. Photo by Steffenie Burns.

"Wanna tell them the good news?" Blankenship grinned gratefully and announced, "I'm on scholarship!" He was immediately mobbed by his teammates.

In retrospect, Georgia turned a corner in South Bend, and not geographically. The program had savvy leadership. If you are flush with the right stuff at the top and that right stuff filters down to the staff and players, momentum can, and should, build.

Already, Kirby and his staff knew that one of the keys to success had manifested itself. The gripping leadership of the four who paused their entry into the NFL was, perhaps, the cornerstone of the success of the 2017 team. Chubb, Michel, Lorenzo Carter and Davin Bellamy were steady to overwhelming playmakers on the field. When the day was done, their maturity about where they went, what they said, what they

Dec. 2, 2017: Georgia 28, Auburn 7, in Atlanta. After being dominated by the Tigers in Auburn in November, the Bulldogs were prepared for a SEC Championship Game performance in Mercedes-Benz Stadium. Georgia dominated the game after Auburn's first possession. Much of that was the result of the play of Roquan Smith, the game's MVP, who had a career-high 13 tackles (10 solos), one sack, two tackles for loss and two fumble recoveries. Another highlight was when D'Andre Swift found a hole to the left side of the line of scrimmage, sprinted through and then outran the defensive backs on an explosive 64-yard run. The Bulldog reserves then ran out the clock for Georgia's 13th SEC title.

Coach Smart and his Dawgs, including defensive MVP Roquan Smith (3), celebrate the first conference title under Smart's leadership. Photo by Steffenie Burns.

BULLDOG

2007-2017

JIM CHANEY:
"Football Fits Here"

There is an art to play calling, which is not an exact science. It can, however, enjoy percentage success, depending on a variety of factors, some of it having to do with the defense being out of position ever so slightly, or an offensive lineman being shaded too much one way or the other—factors not easily recognized by the naked eye belonging to critics from 40 rows up in the stands. Sometimes the defense simply makes a dominating play.

Critics of play calling are like gossip mongers—they are given to flapping their gums ritualistically. It is a spectator's prerogative. You take your seat and settle in, taking on your fault-finding demeanor and begin carping away. Many critics are former players themselves.

Championship teams have fewer critics, mainly because such teams usually line up offensive lines that can pave the way to point production, which brings about victory more often than not. Championship teams field dominating offensive lines. The better the offensive lines, the less carping and complaining.

Nonetheless, it is fashionable to lambast play calling. The media, which most everybody loves to hate, can be accomplices to the routine. This is why most coaches come with the testimony of not reading the newspapers/Internet or watching "SportsCenter."

I have never felt that any of the unwashed can legitimately critique play calling. All, however, are geniuses when it comes to critiquing results. It is difficult for coaches to set the record straight. First and foremost, especially this day and time, a head coach can't throw assistants and players under the bus.

Let's be up front. Coaches do make mistakes, but I have always enjoyed this bit of doggerel.

"To err is human,

"To forgive is divine,

"But to forgive an offensive coordinator is unheard of."

The critics don't bother Jim Chaney, who goes through a self-analyzation of his Georgia offense every week. He second guesses himself, more than the critics. He invites his staff to second guess the game plan (there are post mortems, too). Chaney teaches percentage football, understanding that in this imperfect football world, perfection is seldom achieved. He seeks the advantage for his team by teaching sound fundamental principles, not trying to keep the game from becoming complex. Yet, offensive coordinators must be creative and innovative because defenses are more athletic and more sophisticated than they have ever been.

Chaney loves the play-action game. He has been around, including a stop in the National Football League. He learned in the NFL that "you don't throw it every snap." He would never diminish the importance of the passing game. Throwing the ball is critically important but he is not one of those gunslinging offensive coordinators who is trying to make a name for himself by accumulating a fistful of stats.

There is only one stat that resonates with Chaney—the one that reflects "W."

The aforementioned gunslingers have little or no regard for aiding and abetting the defense. No Georgia fan, up to date on Bulldog history, would fail to sing the praises of the late Erk Russell, the beloved defensive coordinator. Erk was effective at finding a way to shut down prolific offenses, but he was keenly aware that he benefited from Georgia's ball-control offense.

In the last year of his life, I visited Bum Phillips at his ranch in Goliad, Texas. I had come to see him to talk football. He was up to it. Our conversation covered countless topics, and the only time he seemed emotionally piqued was when I asked him what it was like to work with Sid Gillman, whom many say was the ultimate offensive genius.

"Awful," said Bum, the former Chargers defensive coordinator, of his tenure with the San Diego. "He didn't give a damn about defense. The only thing important about defense for him was to get the ball back so he could try some of his fancy offensive wrinkles to try to dazzle the TV analysts. He was in love with offensive statistics. That was the worst job I ever had."

When the offensive coordinator and the defensive coordinator develop a genuinely compatible partnership, a consistency of success is likely to ensue. Chaney's offense features some high-octane plays, but in general, the way he runs the offense does not put pressure on Mel Tucker's defense.

Chaney grew up in Holden, Missouri, which is 50 miles southeast of Kansas City, a farm boy who knows about row crops, picking, fencing, fixing and mending. He learned to drive tractors when he was in grade school. He can tell you all about Allis Chalmers, Farmall and John Deere tractors.

Chaney took to sports early on, but admits up front with a wry grin, "I wasn't very good." Like all who have played football on any level, he remembers the fun he had with his teammates. "Being part of a team has always been uplifting, regardless of the level of the success you achieve," he says. "You learn that no matter the result that you get up and keep going, play after play."

That is, without question, a life lesson testimony that will stand the test of time. The Jim Chaney view is football makes kids realize that championship success can come when the focus is on the team; that the most resonating byproduct of football is that by tirelessly working together, it can bring about emotionally stirring results.

It is the same all across the country. It is the same in Southeast Missouri as it is in South Georgia. Communities bond with Friday Night Lights. Games in Holden might not attract more than 600 people, but everybody in the county loved the Eagles.

While Chaney doesn't give himself high ratings as a player, Central Missouri State (now University of Central Missouri) offered him a full scholarship to play for the Mules. (He was an All-Conference defensive lineman). He remembers the value of the scholarship: $1,900. For a farm boy, that was a big deal. His major was physical education, which would set him on a path to return to a "Friday Night Lights" scene. However, he wanted to broaden his horizons. Following graduation, he lit out for Cal State Fullerton, where he was a graduate assistant enrolled in sports management. That led to his introduction to the hedges of Sanford Stadium. The Titans played between the hedges in 1991 and 1992, losing 27-14 and 56-0, respectively. Playing on the road for a check became standard with Cal State. The Titans would give up football because of financial deficiency.

Chaney was enjoying coaching, despite the budget constraints. He resided in Newport Beach, 24 miles away, which offered good-living fulfillment. He thought about enrolling in law school but landed in Laramie where he became offensive line coach and recruiting coordinator for Wyoming.

The late Joe Tiller took Chaney to Purdue in 1997 where Chaney coached eventual Super Bowl champion quarterback Drew Brees. Except for coaching the St. Louis Rams offensive line for three seasons (2006-08), Chaney has been offensive coordinator at Tennessee, Arkansas and Pittsburgh before coming to Georgia.

Chaney provided his take on Athens and the University of Georgia.

"If you work in college football, you know about the tradition of Sanford Stadium and the hedges. Georgia has an exceptional fan base. Kids like to play here," he says. "Athens is a great place to live. Before you work, you have to live. I love driving to work in the morning. Georgia is a unique place. You know you can be competitive every game. UGA has the resources to compete. Football is important in this state and it is important to this university.

"There are good players in the state, and there is excellent high school coaching. Our players enjoy it here. They love this town and this campus. Football fits here."

JAMES COLEY:
"We Have Never Had It So Good"

When Texas A&M offered James Coley an attractive opportunity following Georgia's Rose Bowl euphoria in January 2018, his emotions experienced an elevated crisis about whether to accept the offer to relocate his family in College Station, Texas, or to stay put in Athens.

His final decision was without anything negative in his thought process about the Aggies and an opportunity to work for new A&M coach Jimbo Fisher, an old friend. However, he would prefer to remain in Athens if he could. Coaches often experience that emotional tug of war when certain job opportunities come about. Career advancement, having to do with responsibility and financial incentive, are reminders that you have to lead with your head and not your heart.

When he got on the plane to fly to College Station, before takeoff, he thought to himself, "It has to be an exceptional offer for me to leave Athens."

His wife, Kenia, was happy. His kids, Madison and Brady, were very happy. In fact, James himself could not have been any happier. He became appreciative of the opportunity in College Station, but he knew he could not go wrong in Athens.

The positives in geographical status quo were as encouraging as possible. He likes working with Kirby Smart, he has an uplifting rapport with the coaching staff and "has never worked at a place with more potential than Georgia." He goes on to say, "Hey man, we can win here, and the fan base is hungry for success. They make us feel that they like us."

The good news is that, in addition to a pay raise, Coley was given a title that resonated with him for his coaching resume: co-offensive coordinator/quarterback coach. While he has a defined recruiting territory like the rest of the staff, in reality, the Coley recruiting map is anywhere there is a great quarterback prospect.

When there was disappointment in Kirby's first year, many grumbled and were not sold on the commitment and versatility of the assistants. I felt that I knew something about them. I have never seen a staff work harder, dating back to Vince Dooley's first staff. Led by Erk Russell and Bill Dooley, that staff was as fundamentally sound as there ever was in Athens. When I am in town, I often work on Saturdays and Sundays. With my office positioned near the front entrance to the building, I not only observed the work ethic, I got a sense of what they were doing, which reflected hospitality, commitment and direction.

Early on when I met James Coley, I knew why Nick O'Leary enrolled at Florida State. Nick's parents, Nan (volleyball) and Bill (football), were letterwinners in Athens. The kid grew up a passionate Georgia fan. His parents asked for a "used" Georgia helmet for his room. Later when we visited the O'Leary's and I walked by Nick's room, there was that helmet, prominently displayed. I had counted on Nick following in his parents' footsteps, but the short answer was that he, for the longest time, wanted to play where his dad played football, but FSU's James Coley got in the way. For sure, the Eskimos would buy ice from Coley.

"When you live in a place like Athens," James says, "and your job is the best fun and your family feels welcomed and is happy in Athens, it would be hard to leave. In the coaching business, you never know where the career road will take you. Kenia and I are happy it has brought us to Athens where we have found the greatest place to live with the greatest coaching opportunity and the greatest fans. We have never had it so good."

preached — even what they drank — resonated with their teammates. That meant this team had potential, it had resiliency, audacity, balance and togetherness. It was opportunistic. It had class and empathy. That is why it became the SEC champion.

From South Bend, the Bulldogs developed into an overachieving team that feared no opponent and respected them all. There was one toe stumping that caused unmitigated carping — the 40-17 loss at Auburn. It was not as bad as it looked, although it was troubling that, for the first time, the Dawgs looked bad.

(Below) With Georgia having gained the advantage against Oklahoma in the College Football Playoff semifinal in the second overtime, you could feel the momentum accumulating for the Bulldogs in the iconic Rose Bowl. Everybody was standing, gripped with anticipation, when quarterback Jake Fromm called for the "Black Susie" play in the huddle—black for the formation and Susie to identify Sony Michel as the ball carrier in the Wild Dawg alignment. Michel was poised to take a direct snap from center. He swept left and there was Fromm shielding a defender, making a key block, and Tyler Simmons and Issac Nauta, sealing off the inside. You know the rest of the story: Lamont Gaillard to Sony Michel to Rose Bowl glory. Photo by Philip Williams.

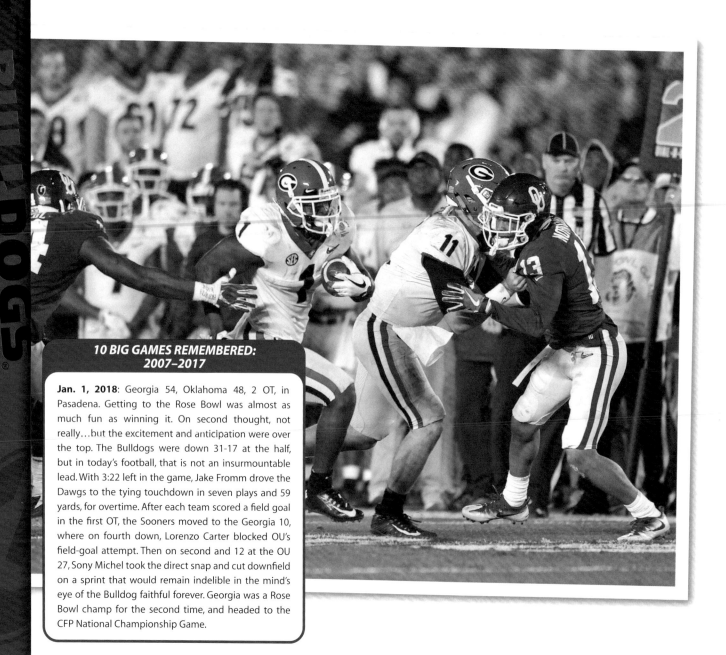

10 BIG GAMES REMEMBERED: 2007–2017

Jan. 1, 2018: Georgia 54, Oklahoma 48, 2 OT, in Pasadena. Getting to the Rose Bowl was almost as much fun as winning it. On second thought, not really…but the excitement and anticipation were over the top. The Bulldogs were down 31-17 at the half, but in today's football, that is not an insurmountable lead. With 3:22 left in the game, Jake Fromm drove the Dawgs to the tying touchdown in seven plays and 59 yards, for overtime. After each team scored a field goal in the first OT, the Sooners moved to the Georgia 10, where on fourth down, Lorenzo Carter blocked OU's field-goal attempt. Then on second and 12 at the OU 27, Sony Michel took the direct snap and cut downfield on a sprint that would remain indelible in the mind's eye of the Bulldog faithful forever. Georgia was a Rose Bowl champ for the second time, and headed to the CFP National Championship Game.

I have long held the view that the longer you tote that No. 1 in the country designation, the heavier it gets. Only three national champs in the last 10 years have finished the season with undefeated records.

The 2017 highlights were innumerable, an artesian flow that seemed to generate nothing but big plays and memorable moments. With Kirby Smart at the controls, there would be more of that in the immediate future.

(Left) Mecole Hardman goes over an Alabama defender on the way to a touchdown in the CFP National Championship Game. Photo by Al Eckford. (Below) Roquan Smith (3) was a brutal force on defense for Georgia during his entire career, but he saved the best for last by racking up 13 tackles against the Crimson Tide, including 2.5 tackles-for-loss. Photo by David Weikel.

10 BIG GAMES REMEMBERED: 2007–2017

Jan. 8, 2018: Alabama 26, Georgia 23, 2 OT, in Atlanta. Remembering a failed objective has no redeeming positives, but that Kirby Smart got Georgia into the CFP National Championship Game in his second season convincingly fuels the belief of the Bulldog Nation that he will have additional opportunities to return to the finals again. Georgia led 13-0 at the half and 20-10 at the end of the third quarter, but failed to score in the final period, which took the game to overtime. In OT, Alabama won with a touchdown to Georgia's field goal. Smart took his lumps like a man and started setting his jaw for the next season.

NEXT: Dawgs back on top. The making of the 2021 national champions. From walk-on to champion. Defensive Dawgs lead the way. Roadblock to a rematch. "Resilient Dawgs" get the confetti in Indy.

Dawgs Back On Top

Stetson Bennett's story will forever resonate with doting alumni. He did not play for an NFL opportunity. He played for glory to old Georgia … His story: From walk-on to the national championship. He will always be a hero in the Bulldog pantheon of players who led his team to a championship.

In only his second year as a head coach, at his alma mater, Kirby Smart took his team to a No. 1 ranking and the national championship game.

Georgia fans were hoping that he would be special, since he had spent 11 years with a close-up view of how Nick Saban managed things at LSU, and Alabama. Kirby collected eight championship rings while at Alabama (four SEC and four national). He also won an SEC ring coaching the running backs at Georgia in 2005.

The main thing he learned to underscore from his time in Tuscaloosa was that recruiting comes first. He realized that nobody recruited with the intensity that Saban did. Saban's view in simple terms was to scout talent better than anybody else, recruit better and recruit for depth across the board.

Kirby incorporated into his approach to coaching a Saban-like-credo and endeavored to work even harder, adding his own twists ensuring that he took the best from his exposure in Tuscaloosa but would be, without question, his own man. That he has succeeded is without debate or disclaimer.

He lobbied for the best facilities. UGA's generous donors stepped up. First came the Payne Indoor Athletic Facility. Then the west end zone expansion came about and following that the Payne expansion with a new weight room, locker rooms, coaches' offices and sports medicine complex — as great as there is on any campus and far better than most.

He lined up the best coaches, analysts and support staff — all subordinated to recruiting the very best players. He took the position that there was no substitute for hard work. He was all about the work ethic. He was not given to social outings and parties. There was no time for small talk. His focus was his work and his football team.

He finds time for his family which leads one to conclude that his focus in life is family and football. You see Mary Beth, Weston, Julia and Andrew on

(Preceding page) Georgia head coach Kirby Smart holds up the College Football Playoff National Championship trophy after the Bulldogs defeated Alabama 33-10 in Indianapolis' Lucas Oil Stadium on Jan. 10, 2022. Photo by Mackenzie Miles. (Right) Since returning to his alma mater for the 2016 season, Smart has led the Bulldogs to two CFP National Championship appearances, four SEC Eastern Division titles, the 2017 SEC title, five bowl victories and 66 wins. Photo by Mackenzie Miles.

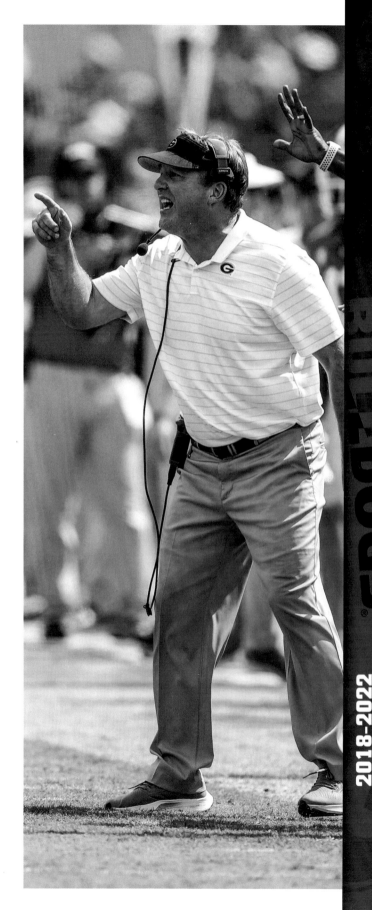

(Above) Quarterback Jake Fromm throws a pass downfield against Auburn in 2018, Fromm threw for 8,224 yards and 78 touchdowns as Georgia's starting QB from 2017-19. His 78 career passing TDs are second in UGA history. Photo by Kristin M. Bradshaw.

Gameday with the greatest of loyalty and respect for the patriarch. His parents, Sonny and Sharon Smart, and Mary Beth's father, Paul Lycett, are often on hand to pitch in and to baby sit.

When he is coaching, priority still goes to recruiting. Everything is subordinated to the goal of bringing the best players to Athens. Before you can be No. 1,

recruiting has to be No. 1. Mastery of the Xs and Os is important, but recruiting is more important than eating and sleeping.

His day is packed with a to-do list in which coaching his football team is never taken for granted. He enjoys golf and quail hunting, for example, but no outside interest ever interrupts his football routine.

His philosophy is old school in that defense still is a priority if you want to win championships. But, you have to also find a way to score, especially in close games. The mental and emotional aspect of the game is always underscored.

The late Bob Neyland, Tennessee's renowned "General Neyland," espoused the view that you can't get a team up for a peak performance more than once, perhaps, twice in a season.

This means that all teams are likely to have an off day. When that takes place against the best competition, you are more likely to lose a game. Saban proved that by recruiting talented depth at every position, he could beat you with talent when his team experienced an off day.

Kirby has the same recruiting mantra, and his indefatigable work ethic had him enjoying recruiting success in his very first year. His first recruiting class was ranked No. 6 and by 2018, he had his first top-ranked recruiting class.

He had prepared himself to be a head coach all along by paying attention to the work of assistant coaches at the schools which Alabama played. For example, he, as Bama's defensive coordinator, was impressed with the size and skills of the Arkansas offensive line, coached by Sam Pittman, who became the Razorbacks head coach in 2020.

Before an Alabama-Arkansas game several years ago, Kirby met up with Pittman pre-game and complimented him on the impressive performance of the Arkansas offensive line. Then, he told Pittman that "when I get a head coaching opportunity, you will be hearing from me."

That confirms that Kirby was laying a foundation that would serve him well when he became a head coach. When he got the job at Georgia, he had a ready list of coaching candidates to choose from. Sam Pittman was one of the first established assistant coaches that he called.

Kirby is on top of everything from office furniture to player development. It took him six years to win his first national championship even though it could have happened in only his second year.

That was his first game against Alabama at the Mercedes-Benz Stadium in Atlanta on Monday, Jan. 8, 2018. Georgia had won the SEC championship by defeating Auburn in the same arena on Dec. 2, 2017.

The painful loss to Alabama in Atlanta was exacerbated by the admission of the Big Ten officials that they had missed several calls. The most critical, a game changer, came when the Bulldogs' Tyler Simmons blocked a Tide punt on fourth and eight at the kicking team's 24-yard line.

Simmons was not offsides, which was a bitter moment for Smart, but you never heard him carp about the bad call.

A year later in the SEC Championship Game in the same stadium, it was another heartbreaker for the Dawgs. Entering the final quarter, Georgia held a 28-21 lead, but the Tide scored two touchdowns in the fourth quarter while the Bulldogs did not score any — Alabama won 35-28.

More disappointment would follow. The Bulldogs lost in Tuscaloosa in the Coronavirus-blighted season of 2020 and then in the '21 SEC championship game in Atlanta. Alabama, with its back to the wall, played its greatest game of the 2021 season and defeated Georgia 41-24. Kirby Smart had gone 0-4 versus the team he helped coach to all those championships.

D'Andre Swift (7) outraces several Auburn defenders during a 77-yard touchdown run in the fourth quarter that iced a 27-10 victory over the rival Tigers in Sanford Stadium in 2018. Photo by Kristin M. Bradshaw.

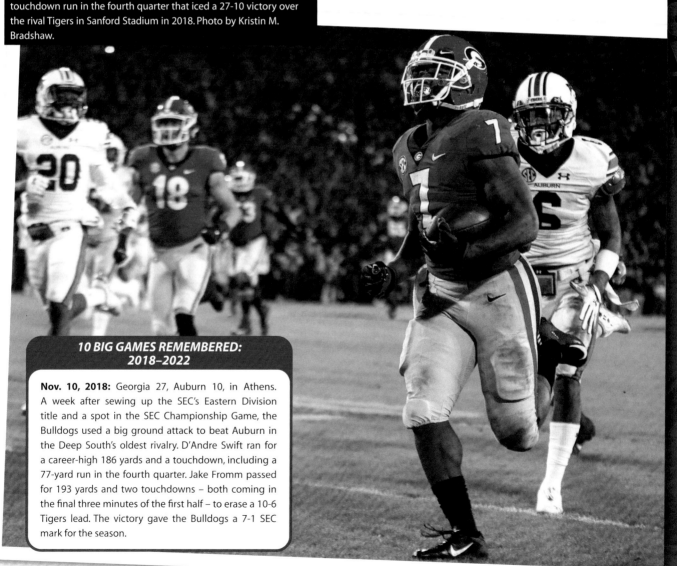

10 BIG GAMES REMEMBERED: 2018–2022

Nov. 10, 2018: Georgia 27, Auburn 10, in Athens. A week after sewing up the SEC's Eastern Division title and a spot in the SEC Championship Game, the Bulldogs used a big ground attack to beat Auburn in the Deep South's oldest rivalry. D'Andre Swift ran for a career-high 186 yards and a touchdown, including a 77-yard run in the fourth quarter. Jake Fromm passed for 193 yards and two touchdowns – both coming in the final three minutes of the first half – to erase a 10-6 Tigers lead. The victory gave the Bulldogs a 7-1 SEC mark for the season.

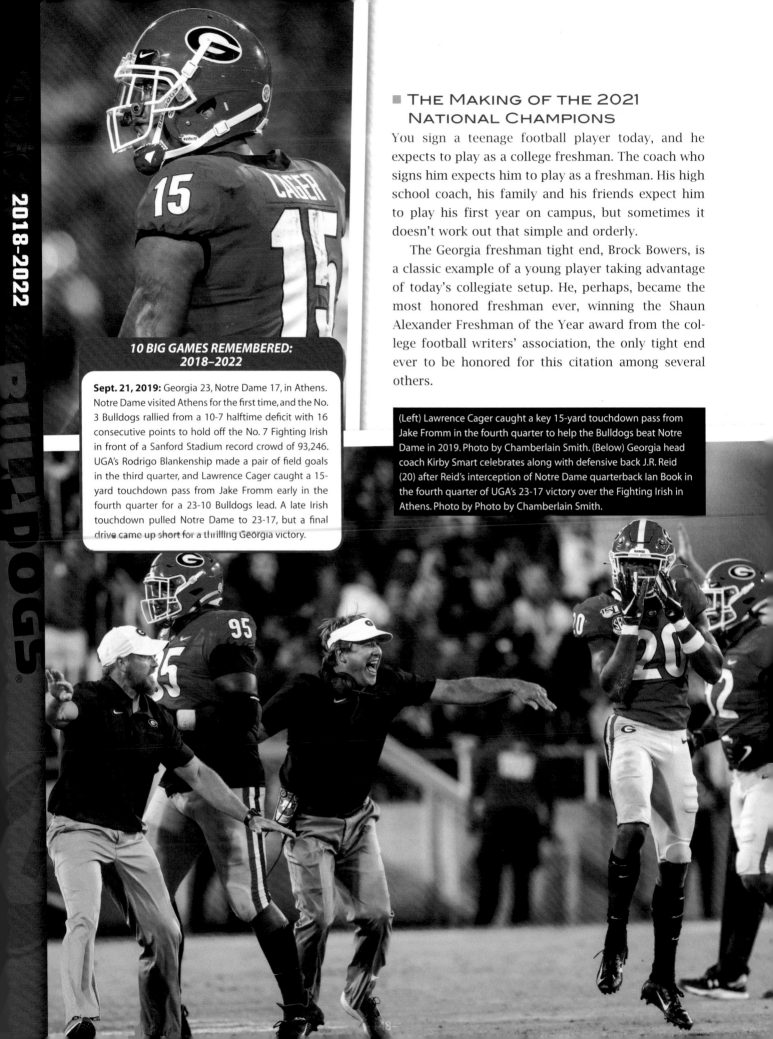

■ THE MAKING OF THE 2021 NATIONAL CHAMPIONS

You sign a teenage football player today, and he expects to play as a college freshman. The coach who signs him expects him to play as a freshman. His high school coach, his family and his friends expect him to play his first year on campus, but sometimes it doesn't work out that simple and orderly.

The Georgia freshman tight end, Brock Bowers, is a classic example of a young player taking advantage of today's collegiate setup. He, perhaps, became the most honored freshman ever, winning the Shaun Alexander Freshman of the Year award from the college football writers' association, the only tight end ever to be honored for this citation among several others.

10 BIG GAMES REMEMBERED: 2018–2022

Sept. 21, 2019: Georgia 23, Notre Dame 17, in Athens. Notre Dame visited Athens for the first time, and the No. 3 Bulldogs rallied from a 10-7 halftime deficit with 16 consecutive points to hold off the No. 7 Fighting Irish in front of a Sanford Stadium record crowd of 93,246. UGA's Rodrigo Blankenship made a pair of field goals in the third quarter, and Lawrence Cager caught a 15-yard touchdown pass from Jake Fromm early in the fourth quarter for a 23-10 Bulldogs lead. A late Irish touchdown pulled Notre Dame to 23-17, but a final drive came up short for a thrilling Georgia victory.

(Left) Lawrence Cager caught a key 15-yard touchdown pass from Jake Fromm in the fourth quarter to help the Bulldogs beat Notre Dame in 2019. Photo by Chamberlain Smith. (Below) Georgia head coach Kirby Smart celebrates along with defensive back J.R. Reid (20) after Reid's interception of Notre Dame quarterback Ian Book in the fourth quarter of UGA's 23-17 victory over the Fighting Irish in Athens. Photo by Photo by Chamberlain Smith.

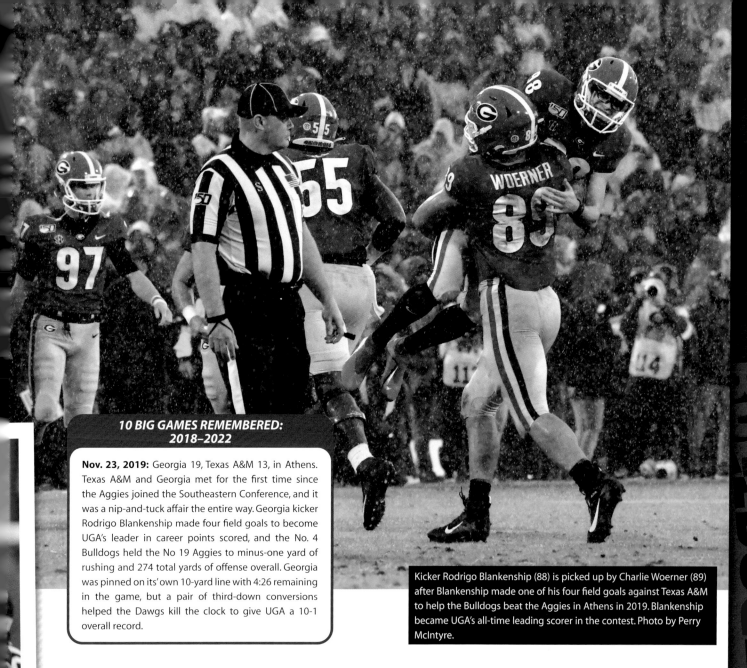

10 BIG GAMES REMEMBERED: 2018–2022

Nov. 23, 2019: Georgia 19, Texas A&M 13, in Athens. Texas A&M and Georgia met for the first time since the Aggies joined the Southeastern Conference, and it was a nip-and-tuck affair the entire way. Georgia kicker Rodrigo Blankenship made four field goals to become UGA's leader in career points scored, and the No. 4 Bulldogs held the No 19 Aggies to minus-one yard of rushing and 274 total yards of offense overall. Georgia was pinned on its' own 10-yard line with 4:26 remaining in the game, but a pair of third-down conversions helped the Dawgs kill the clock to give UGA a 10-1 overall record.

Kicker Rodrigo Blankenship (88) is picked up by Charlie Woerner (89) after Blankenship made one of his four field goals against Texas A&M to help the Bulldogs beat the Aggies in Athens in 2019. Blankenship became UGA's all-time leading scorer in the contest. Photo by Perry McIntyre.

His versatility was gloriously obvious — he could make the big play whether you needed three yards or 30; or a touchdown. He seemed to maneuver into space for big plays, scoring one of 89 yards versus UAB and later went 77 yards, a thing of rare beauty, in the last regular season game versus Georgia Tech. He had six touchdowns of 25 yards or more for the 2021 national champions. Bowers' performance with the Dawgs was as fine as the best wine produced in Napa County where he grew up.

(Had the other tight end, Darnell Washington, not broken his foot, no telling what he might have accomplished. One can only imagine what these two talents might have brought to the table with a healthy Washington in the lineup.)

Conversely, Jordan Davis was not a five-star recruit, but his development at Georgia is a reminder that the collegiate system today has become a godsend for the National Football League. When the colleges send cogent players, with three years of seasoning such as that which kids get from playing in the Southeastern Conference, the NFL literally has no cost of development.

Davis could have left Athens early for the NFL, but made a pact with his best friend, Devonte Wyatt, to return to campus. Both now realize the wisdom on their decisions. A Tar Heel native, Davis, and a Georgia boy, Wyatt, were examples of the brotherly love that aids and abets a team in the making of a champion.

Quarterback Jake Fromm (11) sets to pass behind the Bulldogs' offensive line, including Jamaree Salyer (69) and Warren Ericson (50) against Baylor in the 2020 Allstate Sugar Bowl. Fromm threw for a pair of touchdowns in the victory over the Bears. Photo by Tony Walsh.

10 BIG GAMES REMEMBERED: 2018–2022

Jan. 1, 2020: Georgia 26, Baylor 14, in New Orleans. The No. 5 Bulldogs used a big first half in the Allstate Sugar Bowl to beat the No. 7 Bears. Jake Fromm threw a pair of second-quarter TD passes to freshman wide receiver George Pickens, and UGA got two field goals from Rodrigo Blankenship for a 19-0 lead at halftime. Pickens tied a UGA bowl record with 12 receptions for 175 yards and a touchdown for Sugar Bowl Most Outstanding Player honors.

George Pickens celebrates after catching a touchdown pass from Fromm in the second quarter. Pickens tied a UGA bowl record with 12 receptions against Baylor. Photo by Kristin M. Bradshaw.

One of the most memorable scenes came at the victory celebration in Athens following the title victory in Indianapolis. Jordan (defense) and Jamaree Salyer (offense) — the latter, the bell cow and the mainstay of the offensive line — spoke for the team to the thousands who gathered in the stadium, on the bridge and in the streets adjoining the prettiest facility there is in college football. Jordan, when he concluded his remarks, raised his outer jacket revealing underneath an Atlanta Braves jersey.

When the Braves won the World Series in October while the Bulldogs were ranked No. 1, there was talk of the state's two most favorite teams claiming the ultimate prize in their respective sports.

Ofttimes the most talented team is not the "best" team. Georgia, in 2021, was a very talented team, but it had that bonding ingredient that enabled the Bulldogs to realize their potential because they were selfless and team oriented.

This team was a collection of different personalities and interests with a common goal. Zamir White and James Cook, quiet men, were selfless players who underscored the work ethic and subordinated personal goals to best interests of the team.

Julian Rochester played in the College Football Playoff championship game of 2017 and overcame injuries to stay the course that led to a championship. He took the loss in SEC title game very hard, crying profusely, while sitting in his locker, to joyously exulting triumphally when the game was over in Indianapolis. Nobody enjoyed redemption more than this Powder Springs native.

The walk-on kickers, punter Jake Camarda and placekicker Jack Podlesny performed as expertly as any pair of specialists in the past; Derion Kendrick, who got in trouble at Clemson but redeemed himself with a second opportunity — one of the rare college players to earn a championship ring with two different schools; Nakobe Dean, the model student-athlete with a 4.0 GPA in engineering and good works resume that is off the charts. His story is reminiscent of the all-around heroes of yesteryear.

Two basketball aficionados, Travon Walker and Ladd McConkey, realized their future was in football. Both made noteworthy contributions to the success of the team. McConkey, has a rare ability to get open downfield. Adonai Mitchell with an athletic catch of a Stetson Bennett perfectly thrown ball for a touchdown in the fourth quarter at Indy, was a big play receiver for his team throughout the season.

Georgia partisans will never forget the bookend interceptions that confirms the notion that defense still wins games. Chris Smith's 74-yard interception return in the Clemson game and Kelee Ringo's nail-in-the-coffin 79-yard return in Indianapolis will remain unforgettable as long as the story of the 2021 Bulldog season is told and retold through the years.

10 BIG GAMES REMEMBERED: 2018–2022

Jan. 1, 2021: Georgia 24, Cincinnati 21, in Atlanta. The Chick-fil-A Peach Bowl matchup between the No. 9-ranked Bulldogs and the No. 8-ranked Bearcats went down to the wire as Jack Podlesny hit a career-long 53-yard field goal with three seconds left in the game to complete UGA's rally to the victory. Georgia got a 16-yard TD pass from quarterback JT Daniels and a Podlesny field goal in the first half, but trailed 14-10. Cincinnati led 21-10 early in the third quarter, but it was all Bulldogs the rest of the way as UGA scored the game's final 14 points – all in the fourth quarter.

(Below left): Kicker Jake Podlesny (96) composes himself prior to the snap before he kicks a 53-yard field goal to beat Cincinnati in the 2021 Chick-fil-A Peach Bowl in Atlanta. Holder Jake Camarda (90) looks to Podlesny before he motions for the snap prior to the kick. Photo by Tony Walsh. (Below right): Linebacker Azeez Ojulari (13) celebrates after one of his three sacks of the Bearcats in the Peach Bowl. Georgia's defense recorded eight sacks in the comeback victory over Cincinnati. Photo by Tony Walsh.

Sept. 4, 2021: Georgia 10, Clemson 7, in Charlotte. The Bulldogs opened the season as the No. 5 team in the country, and Georgia faced a stern test with No. 3 Clemson. Late in the first half, a Clemson punt deflected off a Georgia player and was recovered by the Tigers at midfield. Five plays later, Georgia's Christopher Smith intercepted a pass and went 74 yards for the only touchdown of the contest. UGA kicker Jack Podlesny made a 22-yard field goal late in the third quarter for a 10-0 lead, and the only Clemson points came on a field goal midway through the fourth quarter.

(Top) Georgia's Nakobe Dean (17) sacks Clemson quarterback D.J. Uiagalelei (5) in Georgia's 10-7 victory over the Tigers to begin the 2021 season. It was one of two sacks for Dean against Clemson. Photo by Tony Walsh. (Below): Christopher Smith (29) holds the football while teammate Kelee Ringo (5) celebrates after Smith's 74-yard interception return for a touchdown in the second quarter against Clemson. Photo by Tony Walsh.

■ FROM WALK-ON TO CHAMPION

Then there was Bennett — along with Rochester, the greybeards on the team — a little guy quarterback (by today's standards anyway at 5-11, 185 pounds) who took advantage of his assets — competitive heart, quick feet and heady command of the position, insightful decision making — and the spread-out offenses today to where he could find open lanes, mastering the play action passing game to become one of the greatest feel-good stories in history of UGA.

His story will forever resonate with doting alumni. He did not play for an NFL opportunity. He played for glory to old Georgia. However, the name, image and likeness protocol (NIL) rewarded him handsomely as one of five quarterbacks who led the Bulldogs to a national championship. His time, without question, was the best of times.

Stetson, the grandson of a well-known collegiate assistant, Buddy Bennett, who played at South Carolina and coached at his alma mater, Georgia

Tech, and Tennessee, was always cool under fire and in control of his emotions until he realized at Lucas Oil Stadium in Indianapolis that Ringo was going to score and put the game out of reach.

Then he lost it. The tears began to gush forth with alacrity. He felt like a big weight had been lifted from his shoulders. He had taken the slings and arrow of detractors who found fault with him for no discernable reason. He was leading his team to victory. He was a modest, selfless player who put his team and teammates first.

He demonstrated undying love for the University of Georgia, having become a Bulldog by the time he shed his diapers. He played touch games on Herty Field on North campus. He stood by the hedges and watched his heroes in pre-game warmups — quarterback David

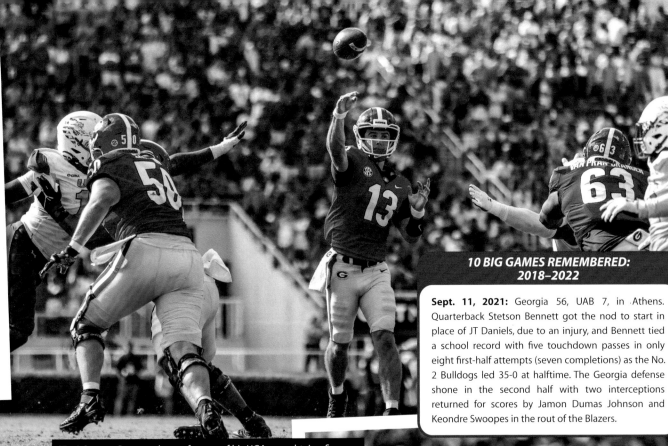

(Top) Stetson Bennett throws for one of his UGA record-tying five touchdowns in a 56-7 rout of UAB in Athens in 2021. Bennett threw his five TD passes in just eight total pass attempts in the first half of the victory over the Blazers. Photo by Mackenzie Miles. (Right) Georgia defensive lineman Jordan Davis fights off UAB linemen in the 2021 victory over the Blazers in Athens. Davis was the 2021 Outland Trophy winner and a first-team All-America choice by several media outlets. Photo by Mackenzie Miles.

Greene, and defensive backs Thomas Davis and Greg Blue. All his life, he wanted to enroll in Athens and play for the Dawgs. It was a highlight when he walked on in 2017 and redshirted.

There was always something about him that resonated. When he was a scout team quarterback, he was adept at giving the varsity defense the look they needed to prepare for the game on Saturday. However, he was pretty much relegated to back-up status which led to a decision to transfer to Jones College in Ellisville, Mississippi, where he flourished, taking his team to a 10-2 record and a win in the Mississippi Bowl and the conference championship game.

However, he longed for Athens and the hedges of Sanford Stadium, so he returned "home." He'd rather be a backup at Georgia than a starter at a lower level, but make no mistake about it, he felt he could win the starting job with the Bulldogs. He played in five games in 2019, started five games in 2020 and 10 in 2021. Once he got the job, he could not be unseated. When he became the incumbent, he never let go.

His story: From walk-on to the national championship. He will always be a hero in the Bulldog pantheon of players who led his team to a championship.

Tight end Brock Bowers (19) leaps to catch a nine-yard touchdown pass from quarterback Stetson Bennett in the third quarter of UGA's 45-0 shutout victory at rival Georgia Tech in 2021. Bowers caught two TD passes in the contest. Photo by Tony Walsh.

■ DEFENSIVE DAWGS LEAD THE WAY

From Labor Day weekend's heat, in the year of the COVID hangover, 2021, Bulldog aficionados in Red & Black caravanned to Charlotte and then throughout the season to end up in the bitter cold of Indianapolis for the National Championship game.

All's well that ends well.

The shortest trip — to Atlanta for the SEC Championship Game — was the only one which left a bad taste in the Bulldog faithful's mouths, but everybody realized there was another tomorrow. The Dawgs would live to fight another day. They were in the playoffs.

From the outset, as has been the case since the serendipitous season of 2017, it has been established that expectations were always going to be high with Kirby Smart in charge at Georgia. Winning the SEC East became a habit, winning it all a greater challenge.

The opening game had significant implications. Clemson, under Dabo Sweeney, had risen to the top as a collegiate power. The Tigers had won two national championships and dominated their league. They had become the class of the Atlantic Coast Conference.

Clemson was ranked ahead of Georgia for this big matchup, and the game was billed as a heavyweight slugfest. The teams were evenly matched, and the final reflected it was a battle royal with the Bulldog

10 BIG GAMES REMEMBERED: 2018–2022

Dec. 31, 2021: Georgia 34, Michigan 11, in Miami Gardens, Fla. The third-seeded Bulldogs faced second seed Michigan in the College Football Playoff Semifinal at the Capital One Orange Bowl, and Georgia used a 17-0 start to cruise to a berth in the CFP National Championship Game. Holding a 7-0 lead, UGA used trickery to double the lead when Kenny McIntosh took a handoff and threw an 18-yard touchdown pass to Adonai Mitchell late in the first quarter. A pair of Jack Podlesny field goals and a 57-yard TD pass from Stetson Bennett to Jermaine Burton extended the UGA lead to 27-3 at halftime. The Georgia defense held the Wolverines, averaging almost 38 points per game, to 11 points, and Derion Kendrick tied a UGA bowl record with a pair of interceptions.

defense having dictated victory with its ability to neutralize the play of Clemson quarterback David "DJ" Uiagalelei.

Georgia's opportunistic defense did not allow a touchdown (Clemson's defense didn't either, by the way). It was fitting that the Bulldog defense won the game, bringing about the reality that this team not only was big and powerful, but it also had a big play defense.

The Tigers got a break when Kendall Milton, midway in the second quarter, fumbled a punt at midfield, where Clemson recovered. Following a Uiagalelei pass completion for a first down, the Tigers faced a third-and-four situation at the Bulldog 40. The next play would become the turning point in the game and also the margin of victory. Chris Smith maneuvered into the path of a Uiagalelei pass and

BULLDOGS

2018-2022

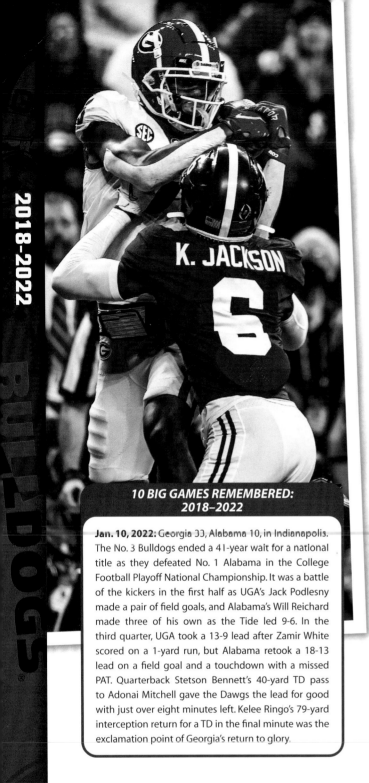

**10 BIG GAMES REMEMBERED:
2018–2022**

Jan. 10, 2022: Georgia 33, Alabama 10, in Indianapolis. The No. 3 Bulldogs ended a 41-year wait for a national title as they defeated No. 1 Alabama in the College Football Playoff National Championship. It was a battle of the kickers in the first half as UGA's Jack Podlesny made a pair of field goals, and Alabama's Will Reichard made three of his own as the Tide led 9-6. In the third quarter, UGA took a 13-9 lead after Zamir White scored on a 1-yard run, but Alabama retook a 18-13 lead on a field goal and a touchdown with a missed PAT. Quarterback Stetson Bennett's 40-yard TD pass to Adonai Mitchell gave the Dawgs the lead for good with just over eight minutes left. Kelee Ringo's 79-yard interception return for a TD in the final minute was the exclamation point of Georgia's return to glory.

(Left) Georgia wide receiver Adonai Mitchell catches a 40-yard touchdown pass from Stetson Bennett over the head of Alabama's Khyree Jackson (6) in the fourth quarter to give the Bulldogs a lead they never relinquished in the College Football Playoff National Championship. Photo by Mackenzie Miles.

In this day of offensive firepower, opponents had trouble scoring on the Bulldog defense from the home opener with UAB through the Georgia Tech game, which turned out to be a coaching clinic in which the Bulldogs' archrival was dominated in slam-dunk fashion.

For the record, here is confirmation that these Dawgs were the class of college football, holding onto the No. 1 ranking from the Auburn game on Oct. 9 to the end of the regular season:

- UAB, in Athens 56-7
- South Carolina, in Athens 40-13
- Vanderbilt, in Nashville 62-0
- Arkansas, in Athens 37-0
- Auburn, in Auburn 34-10
- Kentucky, in Athens 30-13
- Florida, in Jacksonville 34-7
- Missouri, in Athens 43-6
- Tennessee, in Knoxville 41-17
- Charleston Southern, in Athens 56-7
- Georgia Tech, in Atlanta................... 45-0

With Alabama being stressed to win its final game with Auburn on Nov. 27, the SEC showdown matched up the two best teams in the country. That could only happen in the SEC, where "It just means more."

Only in this league could a team win the national championship and not win the league title as was the case this year with Georgia. In 2017, Alabama won the national title and did not win its own division. Auburn won the West that year, but the Tigers lost to Georgia in the SEC Championship Game. Alabama then defeated the Bulldogs in overtime to win the national title.

With its back to the wall, trying to find a way to get into the four-team playoff, Alabama played its best game of the season with Georgia's vaunted defense experiencing a forgettable second quarter in which it surrendered 24 points, and the Crimson Tide upset and outclassed the Bulldogs 41-24.

returned the interception 74 yards for a touchdown and the first points of the game.

Nobody would have bet on it at that time but that was all, as it turned out, that Georgia needed for victory. Each team would score a field goal in the second half of play, but the Bulldogs would hold on or a 10-3 victory and gained traction that would take them to the No.1 ranking and ultimately an undefeated regular season.

■ Roadblock to a Rematch

The Bulldogs returned home embarrassed but resolved to make amends. They wanted another shot at Alabama, quietly confident there would be a different ending.

However, they had to get their priorities in order. Michigan, their first playoff opponent had defeated Ohio State for the first time in years, winning the Big Ten championship and suddenly outranked the Bulldogs in the final poll. The Wolverines could not be taken lightly.

An attitude with the Bulldogs prevailed that it was now the playoff season. Go undefeated in the playoff season and you win the big prize.

The College Football Playoff semifinal took place in Miami, home of the Capital One Orange Bowl Classic, with which Georgia has had a long history. The Bulldogs have played in the Orange Bowl four times

(Above) Georgia defensive back Kelee Ringo (5) speeds down the field during his game-clinching 79-yard interception return for a touchdown in the final minute of the 33-10 victory over Alabama in the 2022 CFP National Championship Game. UGA's Christopher Smith (29) helps to run interference while Alabama's Kristian Story (11) pursues Ringo. Photo by Mackenzie Miles.

over the years, but UGA had an ongoing series with the Miami Hurricanes from the late 1930s through 1966, when Vince Dooley's first SEC championship team lost its only game to the Hurricanes 7-6.

Michigan was a team with a lot of muscle, a fluid quarterback, Cade McNamara, and an iron-fisted defense led by defensive end Aidan Hutchinson, a prime pro prospect. The Wolverines allowed only 16.1 points per game.

The most important factor was the urgency for the Bulldog team to regroup, rebound and regain

momentum. The first drive of the game at Hard Rock Stadium, where the Orange Bowl is now played, confirmed that Georgia was on a mission, that the Bulldogs were bent on redemption.

Bennett directed a flawless scoring drive that reflected complete dominance by the Bulldogs' line of scrimmage, with Bennett hitting tight end Bowers on a nine-yard pass for a touchdown.

That score was followed up by a Kenny McIntosh halfback pass to Mitchell for 18 yards and a 14-0 lead which soon was 17-0 following a Podlesny field goal. Michigan then kicked a field goal, and the Bulldogs were back at it: Podlesny added another field goal, Bennett hit Jermaine Burton on a 57-yard TD pass and then Cook on a 39-yard touchdown pass putting the Bulldogs out front 34-3.

The Dawgs knew early on that they would get their rematch with Alabama. The final score, Georgia 34, Michigan 11.

(Top) Georgia quarterback Stetson Bennett celebrates UGA's national championship victory over Alabama as the confetti falls in Indianapolis' Lucas Oil Stadium. Bennett was named the Offensive Player of the Game after he threw for 224 yards and two touchdowns against the Crimson Tide. Photo by Mackenzie Miles. (Above) Georgia's head coach Kirby Smart (left) is hugged by former UGA head coach Vince Dooley on the field after the Bulldogs beat Alabama 33-10 in the 2022 CFP National Championship Game. Dooley led Georgia to its' last national title after the 1980 season. Photo by Tony Walsh.

■ "Resilient Dawgs" Get The Confetti In Indy

After Alabama slammed Georgia in the SEC Championship Game, the next week, Las Vegas informed the wagering world that Georgia would be favored in the title game to be played at Lucas Oil Stadium in Indianapolis — if there were a rematch.

While the final score in Atlanta might have puzzled the Vegas Society et al, the Georgia players were in agreement. They felt they had played their worst game of the season at the worst time at Mercedes-Benz Stadium the first Saturday in December. Given a second chance, they expected much different results.

They believed in themselves and realized that they had had a bad day. No need to resort to sour grapes, carping and complaining, it was time to set one's jaw and make sure in the rematch that the real Georgia team would stand up.

Both defenses showed up with five field goals and no touchdowns being scored by halftime as Alabama led 9-6. Georgia was shooting itself in the foot on offense, but the defense was keeping Alabama out of the end zone.

The third quarter saw the balance of power begin to shift. Georgia's lines of scrimmage were gaining the edge. The Bulldogs got a break with a Chris Smith interception of Brice Young at the Alabama 43. The 'Dawgs were unable to move the ball, but Carmarda punted dead at the Tide 2-yard line.

Alabama then came with a drive that was spiced with multiple third down conversions, looking ominous and threatful, but the drive stalled at the Georgia 30, where Will Reichard's field goal attempt was blocked by Jalen Carter. Georgia took over at its own 20-yard line, and suddenly the heavens opened. Cook took a handoff, slipped into the Bama secondary, cut to the sideline and sprinted 67 yards to the Tide 13, where three plays later, Zamir White scored from one yard out. Georgia led 13-9.

A Reichard field goal closed the gap to 13-12. Then Bennett was hit trying to get off a pass, and replay ruled it was a fumble, which led to Alabama's scoring drive of 16 yards and a 18-13 lead. It appeared that The Tide had that old magic again, but the "Resilient Dawgs" were far from finished.

Bennett hit Mitchell on a classic throw and catch for a 40-yard scoring play which is akin to what fans are accustomed to seeing on Sunday. That sensational play put Georgia out front 19-18, which would have been enough, but the Bulldogs were bent on slamming the door on Alabama.

A scoring pass of 19 yards from Bennett to Bowers moved Georgia's lead to 26-18, but Young wanted to see his team score and go for two and force overtime.

A funny thing happened at that point to spike Bama's dream. A Young pass not intended for a defender wearing white, was, however, snatched out of the air by Ringo and returned 79 yards for a touchdown, bringing about the final score, Georgia 33, Alabama 18.

The Dawgs were No. 1.

Kirby Smart kisses the CFP National Championship trophy after the Bulldogs defeated Alabama 33-10 in Indianapolis.

ABOUT THE AUTHOR

Loran Smith is a longtime member of the University of Georgia Athletic Department staff who also enjoyed successful careers as a broadcaster, columnist and freelance writer. He spends time at the major golf tournaments, Major League Baseball spring training camps and a number of other popular sporting events and venues, but all are subordinated to his love and interest in the Georgia Bulldogs.

Loran has worked in a variety of jobs with the Bulldogs, from business manager to serving as executive secretary of the Georgia Bulldog Clubs. He was elected to the State of Georgia Sports Hall of Fame in 1997, and has authored or co-authored a dozen books, most of them about the Georgia Bulldogs, including Whitman Publishing's *University of Georgia Football Vault®* and the *Florida-Georgia Rivalry Football Vault®*.

Loran and his wife, Myrna, live a mile from the campus where they met as students. Daughter Camille and son Kent are UGA graduates. The Smiths have four grandchildren: Alex, Zoe, Sophie and Penny.

ACKNOWLEDGMENTS

For sure, it takes a village to put a book together, and the author has many to thank, beginning with Coach Kirby Smart and his staff. From press conferences to bump-ins around the office, to the practice field, to scheduled appointments, there is a gleaning from conversations which allow for insights and vignettes that become a staple of the book.

Thanks also go out to Athletics Director Josh Brooks and Darrice Griffin, Senior Deputy Director of Athletics. The highest of high fives will always be reserved for Claude Felton, Senior Associate Athletic Director/Communications. Claude is highly regarded by his own staff and has the unimpeachable respect of his peers, nationally. He is consumed by his work and is always available whenever needed by those in the media world. And, to a couple of members of his staff, Tim Hix and Leland Barrow for editing and consultation. To Steve Colquitt, who manages the photo department, for his "most valuable" assist in collecting many of the photos in this book. And to photographers Kristin M. Bradshaw, Perry McIntyre, Mackenzie Miles, Chamberlain Smith and Tony Walsh for their great images that are a part of the final chapter of this edition.

Thanks to the Whitman team for making this book possible. Proud to be on your team.

And to my family for their support: My wife, Myrna; daughter Camille, a very fine professional editor and author, and her daughters, Sophie and Penny; My son Kent, who is a devout Bulldog loyalist, his wife, Stephanie, and son, Alex, and daughter, Zoe.

— Loran Smith

UGA FOOTBALL 2021-22:

Coaches:
Kirby Smart..Head Coach
Todd Monken ....Offensive Coordinator/Quarterbacks
Dan Lanning.....................Defensive Coordinator/Outside Linebackers
Glenn Schumann..........Co-Defensive Coordinator/Inside Linebackers
Tray Scott...Defensive Line
Jahmile Addae...Defensive Backs
Matt Luke ....Offensive Line
Dell McGee ....Running Backs
Cortez Hankton..Wide Receivers
Todd Hartley..Tight Ends
Scott Cochran...Special Teams Coordinator
Will Muschamp ....Defensive Analyst/Special Teams Coordinator

Support Staff:
Mike Cavan ....Director of Football Administration
Josh Lee ....Director of Football Operations
Neyland Raper.....................Assistant Director of Football Operations
Jay Chapman.......................................Director of Football Management
Matt Godwin ....Player Personnel Coordinator
Katie Turner ....Director of Recruiting Operations
Christina Harris.......................Director of Recruiting Administration
David Cooper ....Director of Recruiting Relations
Angela Kirkpatrick.....................On-Campus Recruiting Coordinator
Logen Reed ....Assistant Recruiting Coordinator
Cam Lemons.....................................Assistant Recruiting Coordinator
Scott Sinclair ....Director of Strength and Conditioning
Rodney Prince ....Assistant Strength and Conditioning Coach
Ben Sowders ....Assistant Strength and Conditioning Coach
Maurice Sims ....Assistant Strength and Conditioning Coach
Tersoo Uhaa......................Assistant Strength and Conditioning Coach
Buster Faulkner ....Offensive Quality Control
John Jancek... Offensive Quality Control
Robby Discher.....................................Special Teams Quality Control
Bryant Gantt ....Director of Player Programs
Jonas Jennings.....................................Director of Player Development
Austin Chambers ....Assistant Director of Player Development
Juwan Taylor ....Player Development Assistant
Quality Control: Offense – **Montgomery VanGorder, Eddie Gordon, Ryan Williams, Jacob Russell, Rashawn Scott, Stephon Parker;** Defense – **Davis Merritt, Robert Muschamp, David Metcalf, Garrett Murphy;** Special Teams – **Adam Ray, Javi King**
Student Assistants: Offense – **Brandon Bennett, Seth Auer, Jes Sutherland;** Defense – **Blake Bilz, James Ellis**

Football Operations Assistants:
Ron Courson..............................Executive Associate Athletic Director/ Director of Sports Medicine
Drew Willson .... Associate Athletic Trainer
Chris Blaszka.. Assistant Athletic Trainer
Ryan Madaleno .... Assistant Athletic Trainer
Brittany DeCamp... Assistant Athletic Trainer
Connor Norman ....Physical Therapist
Jeremy Klawsky .... Director of Football Technology
Kyle Lane...........................Assistant Director of Football Technology
Solomon Berkovitz..Football Video Intern
Champ Willis..Football Video Intern
Davis Walker...Football Video Intern
Eric Black ....Director of Football Creative
Trevor Terry ....Creative Video Producer
Chad Morehead....................Co-Director of Football Creative Design
Chandler Eldridge ....Co-Director of Football Creative Design
Collier Madaleno.........................Director of Football Player Nutrition
Meaghan Turcotte .... Assistant Director of Football Player Nutrition
Brent Williams...Executive Chef
Ann Hunt ....Administrative Assistant to the Head Coach
Hailey Hughes ....Football Operations Coordinator
Lewis Freeman ....Football Operations Intern
Anna Courson ....Football Operations Intern
John Meshad .... Director of Equipment Operations
Gage Whitten..................Director of Football Equipment and Apparel
Wil Wells...............................Assistant Director of Football Equipment
Roger Velasquez ....Football Equipment Intern